BUCKEYE GLORY DAYS

The Most Memorable Games of Ohio State Football

Eric Kaelin

www.SportsPublishingLLC.com

JM MØ GH JD DG TH DC

Director of production: Susan M. Moyer

Acquisitions editor: Mike Pearson

Developmental editor: Dean Miller

Book design, senior project manager: Jennifer L. Polson

Dust jacket design: Christine F. Mohrbacher

Imaging: Kerri Baker, Christine F. Mohrbacher,
Heidi Norsen, and Kenneth J. O'Brien

Copy editor: Cynthia L. McNew

Photo editor: Erin Linden-Levy

Marketing manager: Cory Whitt

Printed in the United States.

ISBN: 1-58261-681-7

www.SportsPublishingLLC.com

Contents

Preface

When I set out to write this book back in the fall of 2002, I figured that most readers would prefer the "25 Greatest Wins in Ohio State Football History." In theory, it would have been easier to write about the victories. But the more I started asking questions about certain games, the more I began to wonder about including some of the heartbreaking losses as well. Isn't that what being a fan is all about? To fully enjoy the big victories, you have to have suffered a few major defeats along the way. While always a huge showdown, the revenge game of 1970 between Ohio State and Michigan was that much bigger due to the Wolverines' upset of 1969.

Researching and interviewing those who played and covered the games was enlightening to say the least. I had covered Ohio State for the last 10 seasons before delving deep into past games. The Columbus Public Library provided the microfilm, which enabled me to look closely at the build up of each contest, followed by some of the postgame quotes as written by the *Columbus Dispatch*.

The best part of writing the book was getting the chance to sit down and speak with various players from both teams. Whether it be a Heisman Trophy winner or the player who is remembered for only one play in his career, good or bad, it was an honor to have them take time out of their busy schedules to reflect back on a certain game or games.

Late in September of 1993, my wife, Amanda, and I decided to leave Champaign, Illinois, for a job offer with WBNS-AM in Columbus, Ohio. WBNS-AM was moving from an easy-listening station that carried Ohio State football to the only local sports station in Columbus. One of my first duties was to cover then-Ohio State football coach John Cooper's weekly press luncheons. Not knowing where to sit after selecting from the buf-fet luncheon, I stood looking where to sit down to eat. Right away, former play-by-play announcer Bert Charles looked at me and said: "Hey, Red, you can sit here if you want. That's if you don't mind sitting around a couple of old guys like us." Little did I know that the other "old guy," as Bert described it, was none other than legendary Ohio State broadcaster Marv Homan. I figured that if they were kind enough to let me sit down and eat, I should accept.

In talking with Bert, I found out that he had saved boxes of old reel-to-reel tapes of some of the important Ohio State games from the late 1960s until his retirement in 1981. I asked if I could make copies of those broadcasts, which he agreed to, if I would make a copy for his grandchildren as well.

In 2002, Bert learned he had cancer. He did-n't try to hide it and tackled it head on with vigor. I would occasionally take him out to lunch to see how he was doing. Like anyone battling that terrible disease, Bert had his good and bad days, but to Bert, every day he was alive was a good day. Since he liked Chinese food, we often went out to get egg rolls and fried rice. He missed drinking his martinis, so I made sure I drank one for him. In March of 2003, Bert passed away. Although I knew him for only 11 years and was about 45 years younger, I believe there was a mutual admiration between us. He never treated me like a kid and was always giving me tips on life. His tremendous energy, personality, respect for others and charity work will be missed by all who knew him.

In the summer of 2003, Marv Homan came in the studios of WBNS-AM for the re-broadcast of the 1950 Snow Bowl. Former OSU players Dick Logan and Bob Momsen joined us, as did former Michigan player Chuck Ortman. Afterwards, my partner Jack Park and I took Marv out to eat for dinner and were entertained for an hour with his stories about Woody Hayes. Marv is truly a wonderful man who never said anything negative about another person in his life.

Although they don't realize it, their love of talking about past Ohio State football games during Coach Cooper's luncheons, along with the fact that Bert had recordings of some of the games, inspired me to write this book.

The hard part was finding actual audio tape of many of the Ohio State games. Prior to the mid-1980s, stations either threw away or recorded over previous games. Although a few things remain from the 1940s, I decided to start off with the 1954 season. That was Woody's first dominant season.

It would have been easier for me to compile what I felt were the 25 most memorable games. Instead, I decided to put together what I considered a blue-ribbon panel. Looking for an ideal mixture of present-day reporters, along with those who watched games played some 50 years ago, I chose the following: Former OSU sports information director and broadcaster Marv Homan, along with historian Jack Park, were chosen to help make sure that some of the great games from 1954 to the present were not forgotten. Then, reporters Bruce Hooley of the *Plain Dealer*; Tim May from the *Columbus Dispatch*; Rusty Miller of the Associated Press along with Steve Helwagon from Bucknuts.com (formally of the *Buckeye Sports Bulletin*) were picked to help balance out games from the last 20 years. I also wanted a former player's input and selected former running back and author Larry Zelina.

For five months, I wrestled with what games to select. Every time I wrote down my list, I would say to myself, "How did you forget that game?" So I would start over and write my list again and again.

The poll was tabulated much like the weekly writers' or coaches' poll is done. If a game was voted 25th, it received one point. If a game was voted number one, it received the maximum number of points allowed, 25. Each poll was vastly different. Some of the games were easy to choose; most were not. I made an executive decision on one game and one game only. The 1978 Gator Bowl was voted as the 16th greatest game. I decided to leave it out for several reasons. We all know what happened that night between Coach Hayes and Clemson linebacker Charlie Baumann. Although the television captured the hit, no radio recordings exist of the game and most former players didn't want to relive that tragic moment some 25 years later.

Was it a great game? No. Was it a memorable game? Yes, in the sense that a wonderful, yet complex man's legacy will be forever known for "the hit." Whenever a national broadcaster speaks about Hayes, they always talk about Woody losing it on the sidelines. While it was a sad ending, most forget that he "paid forward" more than just about anyone reading this book. I'm not trying to dodge that night; I just felt that there were better "games" to relive.

Finally, I hope this book and CD give you a chance to remember and reflect on all that makes Ohio State football so special. It's been a privilege to report and write about something so great. Go Bucks!

Acknowledgments

While it was a tremendous challenge to write my first book, it was also a lot of fun. How bad can life be when you're sitting down talking to absolutely fantastic people such as Archie Griffin, Hop Cassady, John Hicks, Rex Kern, Jim Lachey, Jim Karsatos and company? I would like to thank all of the former players who took time out to help.

For my buddy, Chris Spielman, thanks for your friendship and giving me the opportunity to sit in and co-host your daily show for the past four years. Your love and passion for the game of football are second to none.

One more former player I would like to mention is quarterback Dave Leggett, who helped lead the Buckeyes to the 1954 national championship. Although it had been 50 years since he played, Dave's memory was like a steel trap, and he was able to relate some wonderful memories. I had a blast just listening to his stories about Woody, Hop and the rest of his teammates.

Projects like these are never possible without the assistance of great people. First, I would like to thank my general manager at WBNS-AM, Dave Van Stone, for allowing me to fulfill a dream and also to use our fantastic new facilities to record the CD. Chief engineer Ron McGrew, along with assistant Jason Knapp, put in some beautiful new equipment while helping me at every turn. Thanks guys!

We value the permission granted by the *Columbus Dispatch* for allowing me to reprint some of the great postgame quotes.

A big thanks to those who allowed me to use their school's radio highlights: sports information directors Tim Tessalone at USC, along with Bruce Madej at the University of Michigan; Oklahoma University assistant athletic director Rick Hart; program director Van Harden and legendary broadcaster Jim Zabel at WHO-Radio in Des Moines, Iowa; Phil Haddy, sports information director at the University of Iowa; John Prosick of WOSU-TV; Kelly Driver and Todd Reigle of WBNS-AM; Sonny and Chance Brockway; and Jeff Brehm of *Buckeye Sports Bulletin*.

It was a pleasure talking over the phone several times with Tom Ufer, son of the late Bob Ufer. Tom, your dad's calls were wonderful! I'm sorry I didn't have the chance to meet him. I know he was special. Thanks for allowing us to use some of his fantastic calls.

I would like to give a special thanks to Jack Park and Bruce Hooley. Their friendship and help have been tremendous. Thanks for looking over my work and guiding me down the right path.

My thanks to the Voice of the Buckeyes, Paul Keels, for the fantastic job he did narrating the CD along with engineer Bob Taylor for long hours putting the whole thing together. I wanted to make sure I had the best possible narrator and engineer/producer for the job and was lucky enough to find both.

I would be remiss in not mentioning Mike Pearson of Sports Publishing L.L.C. for believing in me and allowing me to do this project.

Of course, none of this could be possible without the love and support of my wife, Amanda, along with my sons, Will and Luke. Both are diehard Buckeye fans and encouraged me month after month to complete the book. Without my beautiful wife's support, I could have never gotten through this. Despite the fact that she is a graduate of Indiana University, I still love her.

I would also like to thank my parents, Dick and Ruth Kaelin, my sister Heidi, brother-in-law Scott, nephew Evan and niece Allie and my in-laws, Dick and Veronda Cottle, along with Bill and Moria Cottle. You're only as good as those around you, and their support was tremendous.

It's been a blast writing and recording the book. I hope you enjoy reading it and listening to the *Buckeye Glory Days: The Most Memorable Games.*

—**Eric Kaelin**

BUCKEYE GLORY DAYS

The Most Memorable Games
of Ohio State Football

2002

OHIO STATE 10, PURDUE 6

Heading into Jim Tressel's second season as head coach of the Ohio State Buckeyes, no one could have predicted the success that would await them in 2002. The Buckeyes returned 12 starters and 43 lettermen to a team that had gone 7-5 in 2001. One of the most talked-about freshman classes since 1967 joined the team, led by Mr. Football in the state of Ohio, running back Maurice Clarett. No one knew what to expect out of the offense in 2002. Junior quarterback Craig Krenzel beat out Scott McMullen for the starting job of calling the signals. Only three starters returned on the offensive line.

The Buckeyes' major challenge included replacing its entire offensive backfield, two linebackers and both defensive cornerbacks. A pair of four-year starters returned at the safety positions, two-time All-American Michael Doss along with Donnie Nickey.

The Buckeyes opened their 2002 campaign on a hot and humid August 24 afternoon in Ohio Stadium against Texas Tech. Clarett became the first freshman to start at running back at OSU since WWII as he rushed for an impressive 175 yards and three touchdowns. The Buckeyes then beat Kent State (51-17) and Washington State (25-7) before surviving a close one at Paul Brown Stadium in Cincinnati over the Bearcats 23-19. Ohio State then returned home on October 5 and beat Indiana

(45-17) before winning a night game in Evanston against Northwestern 27-16. San Jose came to Columbus on October 12 for homecoming as OSU beat up the Spartans 50-7. The following week, OSU returned to Big Ten play by winning at Wisconsin 19-14. In that game, Clarett injured his left shoulder, which would affect him the rest of the season. Penn State came to Ohio Stadium on October 26, as the Buckeyes hung on to beat the Nittany Lions in a low-scoring but exciting contest, 13-7, before clobbering Minnesota at home, 34-3.

As Ohio State practiced in the week leading up to the game at Purdue, the coaching staff was keeping a close eye on Clarett. On his weekly call-in show on the Ohio State Football Radio Network, Tressel told announcer Paul Keels and color analyst Jim Lachey: "You never know about shoulders. It's a problem with a nerve, called a stinger. It caused Maurice's left shoulder and arm to go numb. If he's ready to go on Saturday, he could last all day and be fine, or on the first carry get hit the wrong way and get it pinched again. You never know."

While the coaching staff awaited the verdict from the team medical personnel, Coach Tressel announced that senior receiver Chris Vance would not make the trip to Purdue. Vance's brother, Percy Burton, 21, had been shot to death after allegedly shooting another man in a Fort Meyers, Florida, nightspot. The

OPPOSITE: OSU MLB Matt Wilhelm brings down Purdue quarterback Brandon Kirsch. (Jeff Brehm)

other man also died. Despite learning of his brother's death hours before the Minnesota game, Vance chose to play and caught a touchdown pass in the win over the Gophers.

Both Ohio State and Purdue were dealing with injuries to major players. Clarett had sat out the last two games. Purdue freshman quarterback Brandon Kirsch was coming off a broken finger from a fraternity fight and had traded in his fiberglass cast for a brace four days before the game. Even with backup Kyle Orton, Purdue was ranked ninth in the nation and first in the Big Ten in total offense, with an average of 449.3 yards per game. They would be facing an Ohio State defense that was leading the Big Ten in total defense at 305.6 yards per game. In fact, OSU had given up only 291 total yards in its previous two games in wins over Penn State and Minnesota. In both games, wide receiver Chris Gamble started at cornerback. Gamble became the first OSU player to start both offensively and defensively in the same game since Tom Campana in 1971.

On November 9, 2002, Ohio State hit the road for its contest in West Lafayette, Indiana, against Purdue. At 10-0, Ohio State had moved up to second in the latest BCS standings and third in both polls. Purdue entered the game fighting to stay alive for a possible bowl game with a 4-5 record, having lost the five games by a combined total of 22 points. A cloudy, windy afternoon greeted the crowd of 65,250 at Ross Ade Stadium. The Boilermakers opened the scoring in the first quarter as kicker Berin Lacevic booted a 21-yard field goal for a 3-0 Purdue lead. Ohio State's offense was unable to get anything going until seconds before halftime. Facing a third and nine from Purdue's 12-yard line, OSU burned its final timeout to talk things over. It would seem that the Buckeyes had

time for only one pass play, either into the end zone or a sideline pass to a receiver headed out of bounds, but quarterback Craig Krenzel inexplicably ran up the middle and stopped a yard short of a clock-stopping first down. With 12 seconds left, the field goal unit ran onto the field as long snapper Kyle Andrews somehow got off the snap with less than a second remaining. Kicker Mike Nugent converted for his 22nd consecutive field goal as the Buckeyes went into the half tied at 3-3.

Early in the fourth quarter, Purdue quarterback Brandon Kirsch completed a 58-yard pass to flanker Ray Williams on a busted deep coverage before being knocked out of bounds by safety Donnie Nickey. The 58-yard play would be the longest play from scrimmage that an opponent would have all season against the stout OSU defense. Five plays later from the Ohio State four-yard line, senior middle linebacker Matt Wilhelm sacked Kirsch for a six-yard loss back to the 10-yard line. Purdue then settled for a 32-yard field goal by Berin Lacevic as they retook the lead at 6-3. Ohio State defensive coordinator Mark Dantonio would later describe Wilhelm's sack by telling the *Columbus Dispatch:* "That was probably the play of the game. The defense gave them three instead of a touchdown at a critical part of the game."

Late in the fourth quarter, still trailing 6-3, Ohio State's offense took over at its 46-yard line in a final attempt to either win the game or at least force overtime. With Clarett having gone out early in the third quarter after reinjuring his shoulder, the Buckeyes took to the air. On third and 14 from midfield, Krenzel found tight end Ben Hartsock for a 13-yard pickup, a yard shy of a critical first down. It was do or die time for Ohio State. If they couldn't pick up the first down to keep the drive alive, Purdue would take over and run

"I saw **the quarterback scrambling to the right** and I acted like I was with the one receiver so he'd throw it to the other receiver. I timed it right, and it was like the quarterback was throwing it to me as a receiver."

—OSU cornerback Chris Gamble

out the clock for the victory. A loss by Ohio State would ruin a possible perfect season and any shot at contending for the national championship.

On fourth and one from Purdue's 37-yard line with only 1:43 remaining, Krenzel pulled off one of the most memorable plays in Ohio State history. Instead of running a quarterback sneak or throwing a quick pass to tight end Ben Hartsock, Krenzel barely avoided being dragged down by Purdue's blitz, hitting receiver Michael Jenkins on an amazing 37-yard touchdown pass. Mike Nugent nailed the extra point as Ohio State grabbed its first lead of the day at 10-6 with only 1:36 left in the game. When asked afterwards by the *Columbus Dispatch* what play they had run on the touchdown pass, Krenzel replied: "King-right-64-shallow-swat. It was a pass, with the thought of maybe scrambling for the yard for the first down if it was there and no one was open." With tight end Ben Hartsock covered and receiver Chris Gamble running a 15-yard dig route from the right, Krenzel said: "On the snap, the guy pressed Mike [wide receiver Michael Jenkins], and Mike ended up going outside the corner instead of getting inside and running the post over the middle. I just saw that, adjusted to it and put the ball there."

In one final, desperate attempt, Purdue tried to come back. Boilermakers receiver Taylor Stubblefield appeared to be open deep,

but OSU cornerback Chris Gamble raced over and picked off his fourth pass of the season at the OSU 11-yard line with just 45 seconds left to play. The Buckeyes would run out the clock and hold on for a 10-6 victory. Gamble later told Todd Jones of the *Columbus Dispatch*: "I saw the quarterback scrambling to the right and I acted like I was with the one receiver so he'd throw it to the other receiver. I timed it right, and it was like the quarterback was throwing it to me as a receiver."

For Purdue cornerback Antwaun Rogers, getting beat on the touchdown pass was a tough pill to swallow. Not only did it cost Purdue a victory, but his pride as well. Rogers and Jenkins had known each other since they were teammates while playing on the same youth-league football team in the Cincinnati suburb of Forest Park. Rogers was quoted by the *Columbus Dispatch:* "I'm going to hear about this one. I just got to take it like a man for a year," Rogers said with a shy smile. "He made a play. I'll take it."

Coaches always say that championships are won with great defenses. Ohio State came up with three interceptions while holding a powerful Purdue offense to only six points. Matt Wilhelm finished with 6.5 tackles, bringing his team-leading total to 84. He intercepted a pass, setting up the Buckeyes' first field goal while sacking Kirsch on a critical third and three at the OSU four-yard line. Safety

Donnie Nickey saved a potential Purdue touchdown by tackling Williams at the OSU 22-yard line following a 58-yard reception. Doss, who had been victimized two years prior in West Lafayette on a 64-yard touchdown pass to Seth Morales with 1:55 left to win the game for Purdue, came through with a team-leading eight tackles. Gamble picked off his fourth pass of the season to preserve the victory as OSU improved to 11-0 overall and 6-0 in the conference.

Offensively, Krenzel completed 13 of 20 passes for 173 yards, one interception along with the dramatic touchdown pass to win the game. Receiver Michael Jenkins, who caught the touchdown pass, ended up with five receptions for 87 yards on the afternoon. Clarett rushed for 52 yards on 14 carries before leaving early in the third quarter after reinjuring his left shoulder, which had caused him to miss the previous two games.

The Buckeyes were on a roll, and for the first time in years, luck seemed to be on their side. In 1975, 1979, and 1995, Ohio State won its first 11 games before losing. The Buckeyes could improve to 12-0 for the first time in team history with a victory at Illinois the fol-lowing week. Later that same day, after the Buckeyes returned home to Columbus, number one Oklahoma lost a stunner at Texas A&M, 30-26. Ohio State moved up to number one in the BCS standings released that Monday night. The following week, OSU won its first ever overtime game, beating Illinois in Champaign, 23-16, before winning a thriller at home over Michigan, 14-9. Ohio State would then go a perfect 14-0 by topping the Miami Hurricanes in the Fiesta Bowl for the national championship, 31-24 in double overtime.

The panel voted the Buckeyes' 10-6 win at Purdue as the 25th most memorable game in Ohio State football history in the past 50 years.

SCORES BY QUARTERS	1ST	2ND	3RD	4TH	TOTAL
Ohio State	0	3	0	7	10
Purdue	3	0	0	3	6

1st Q-(PUR) Lacevic 21-yd FG (3-0 PUR)
2nd Q-(OSU) Nugent 22-yd FG (3-3)
4th Q-(PUR) Lacevic 32-yd FG (6-3 PUR)
4th Q-(OSU) Krenzel to Jenkins 37-yd TD (10-6 OSU)

1955

OHIO STATE 17, MICHIGAN 0

Many former Buckeyes will tell you that the 1955 Ohio State win at Michigan is one of the greatest victories of all time, period!

Coming off the perfect 10-0 national championship season of 1954, which included a Rose Bowl win over USC, many predicted great things for OSU. Despite the loss of seven senior starters from the 1954 squad, the team returned senior halfback Howard "Hopalong" Cassady along with one of the premier offensive lineman of all time, Jim Parker.

Ohio State opened the 1955 season with a home victory over Nebraska before having its two-season winning streak of 11 snapped by Stanford, 6-0. OSU then beat conference rival Illinois before losing a nonconference game to Duke, 20-14. The Buckeyes rebounded with Big Ten victories over Wisconsin, Northwestern, Indiana and Iowa, setting the stage for a showdown at Michigan.

In what was becoming an annual event, the Big Ten title was on the line as the Buckeyes traveled to Ann Arbor. Ohio State was 5-0 in the conference, while the Wolverines were 5-1. UM could capture the Big Ten title and a trip to Pasadena with a victory over OSU since Michigan played seven league games to the Buckeyes' six.

It would be a bittersweet victory for Ohio State if they beat the Wolverines due to the Big Ten's "no-repeat" rule at that time. An OSU win over Michigan would send second-place Michigan State to the Rose Bowl for the second time in three seasons. MSU had finished conference play the previous Saturday and were scheduled to play Marquette in a season ending nonconference game. So even though OSU would not go out west with a win, a victory would keep its archrival from going.

On Saturday, November 19, 1955, in what was at the time the largest crowd ever to witness a game at a college-owned stadium, 97,369 fans jammed into "The Big House." Nearly three inches of snow had fallen the night before. It took several hundred men to clear the field and seats for Michigan's 600th football game.

The Buckeyes scored first in the second quarter as Fred Kriss, a reserve end from Texas, attempted and completed the first field goal of his career to give the Buckeyes a 3-0 lead. Kriss's line drive boot hit the left upright and bounced in for what would turn out to be the only points OSU would need that day.

OSU continued to hold its 3-0 lead early into the fourth quarter before Cassady ran over a pileup on the right side for a touchdown. Don Sutherin's extra point failed as the score remained 9-0. Ohio State head coach Woody Hayes, in his never-ending attempts to confuse Michigan, had switched Cassady from his normal left halfback position to right half-

OPPOSITE: Ohio State offensive lineman Jim Parker leads the way for Hop Cassady when OSU hosted UM in 1954. (Ohio State University Photo Archive)

ABOVE: Howard Cassady (second from right), along with head coach Woody Hayes (second from left), attends the 1955 Heisman Trophy awards ceremony in December of 1955. (Ohio State University Photo Archive)

back while moving Don Sutherin from the right to left halfback. The move worked. Sutherin, who hadn't carried the ball the previous eight games, went for 75 yards on 18 carries. Fullback Don Vicic carried 17 times for 81 yards and a touchdown. Hopalong Cassady showed why he was the leading candidate for the 1955 Heisman Trophy Award, rushing for 146 yards and a touchdown on 28 carries.

With 2:11 left in the final period, OSU end Bill Michael correctly read a Michigan flat pass and crushed Michigan halfback Terry Barr down in the end zone for a safety, giving the Buckeyes an 11-0 advantage.

Michigan All-America end Ron Kramer attempted an onside kick and barely touched the ball, which OSU recovered at UM's 21-yard line. Four plays later, tempers flared as the Wolverines began to lose their cool. Several unsportsmanlike penalties were called on both sides, with Wolverines Kramer and Michigan tackle Al Sigeman both being ejected from the game for fighting. At the 2004 Columbus Touchdown Club dinner honoring former Ohio State and Michigan players, Kramer said:

"I was trying to strip the ball when the referee threw me out of the game. I think he thought I was trying to hit Cassady, but I was really trying to strip the ball."

On the next play, OSU's Don Vicic busted over the goal line for six more points. Sutherin again missed the extra point as the score stayed at 17-0.

With 1:15 left, OSU kicked off one final time to Michigan. Despite the fact that penalties were being assessed on almost every play, the Wolverines drove the ball to OSU's seven-yard line. As the clock began to wind down, the crowd ran out onto the field. However, Michigan had called a timeout with two seconds remaining as officials pushed the spectators back to the sidelines.

Backup quarterback Jim Van Pelt completed a two-yard pass to the five-yard line as time expired. Ohio State won a convincing 17-0 victory, its second consecutive Big Ten championship along with the first victory in Ann Arbor since 1937. It was the first time since Chic Harley's 1917 squad that OSU had successfully defended the Big Ten championship.

Ohio State's fans uprooted the north goal post and presented it to the flabbergasted players on Michigan's bench. Frustrated Michigan fans joined the OSU fans and players on the field as fists and snowballs flew at various spots around the field. Luckily, few injuries were reported.

Afterward, the *Columbus Dispatch* reported that Woody Hayes wept unashamedly in the locker room and declared: "This is the greatest team I've ever coached. I never saw a team play so close to perfection. You never let up." The team let out a roar and carried Hayes into the showers. After he emerged from the showers, the media asked Hayes if this was a better team than last season's national championship squad. The coach, dripping wet, toweled off his head and insisted: "No, today this was the greatest team I ever coached."

With the, 17-0 victory, OSU became only the second Buckeye team in history to successfully defend the Big Ten championship as they finished up at 7-2. Michigan head coach Bennie Oosterbann, gracious even in defeat, said: "They beat us to the punch."

Coaches say that championships are won with defense. The 1955 Buckeyes were no different. Ohio State had captured the Big Ten championship by holding Michigan to zero points and only 95 total yards on the day. On the season, OSU allowed only 10 points per game while shutting out two opponents.

Typically, the Ohio State-Michigan contest is one of the cleanest-fought contests of the season. Not on this day, however. The *Columbus Dispatch* reported Cassady saying afterwards: "I never played in such a dirty game in my four years at Ohio. They tried to break my leg by twisting it at the bottom of a pile following a tackle late in the game. We stuck to playing football, and that's how we won. Michigan lost their poise."

With OSU beating Michigan and the "no-repeat" rule in effect, the Buckeyes could not defend their Rose Bowl championship. After wrapping up their Big Ten season a perfect 6-0 and with Michigan at 5-2, the 5-1 Michigan State Spartans represented the conference in Pasadena, California. That same day, the Spartans beat Marquette, 33-0, in a non-conference game to finish up at 8-1. At times, the game on the field had to be stopped because of the noise of the crowd screaming over favorable developments of the OSU-UM game.

The 1955 Buckeyes had defeated Michigan for the first time in nine visits to Ann Arbor. In the process, they beat up a Wolverine team that had been rated preseason Big Ten favorite and had only lost once in eight starts. Ohio State's win clinched its second consecutive Big Ten title and kept Michigan from going to the Rose Bowl. After looking at the films on Sunday, Hayes admitted in the *Dispatch* that he was surprised by the Buckeyes' total domination of the game: "I honestly didn't believe that one good team could do that to another good team," he declared. "And we did it all on four plays, just four plays."

The following Monday night at the Ohio Union, more than 1,200 "Appreciation Banquet" guests showed up to cheer on the 1955 Big Ten champions. Cassady was the unanimous choice for the squad's Most Valuable Player. Cassady, Vargo and Parker were all named to the Associated Press All-Big Ten football team for 1955. Cassady would go on in December to win the Heisman Trophy Award, joining former Buckeyes Les Horvath and Vic Janowicz.

For a season that started off at 2-2, an outright Big Ten championship along with one of the greatest OSU wins ever at Michigan seemed to soothe the nerves in Columbus, at least until the fall of 1956.

SCORES BY QUARTERS	1ST	2ND	3RD	4TH	TOTAL
Ohio State	0	3	0	14	17
Michigan	0	0	0	0	0

2nd Q-(OSU) Kriss 20-yd FG (3-0 OSU)
4th Q-(OSU) Cassady 2-yd TD (Ex. Point failed 9-0 OSU)
4th Q—(OSU) Michael tackled Barr in the end zone for a two-point safety (11-0 OSU)
4th Q-(OSU) Vicic 2-yd TD (Ex. Point failed 17-0 OSU)

1974

OHIO STATE 12, MICHIGAN 10

Woody Hayes and Bo Schembechler were at the heart of the "Ten-Year War" as Ohio State and Michigan battled it out once again in 1974 for the Big Ten title. In the first five years of head-to-head battles between Woody and Bo, both teams had earned a 2-2-1 record. The tie had come the previous season in Ann Arbor. Michigan entered the contest 10-0 overall, 7-0 in Big Ten play. The Buckeyes were 9-1 on the season, including a 6-1 mark in the conference. If Michigan beat or tied Ohio State, the Wolverines would represent the conference in the Rose Bowl. If the Buckeyes won, the schools would tie for the championship, forcing the conference athletic directors to fly to Chicago the following day and vote to see which team should play in Pasadena. Following the tie in 1973, the athletic directors surprisingly voted 6-4 in favor of Ohio State to play on New Year's Day.

As one might expect, the pressures of coaching at either school are enormous. The night before the 1970 Rose Bowl, Schembechler suffered a heart attack and turned over his coaching duties to assistant Jim Young. While Schembechler recovered, his Wolverines lost to USC. In June of 1974, the 61-year-old Hayes suffered his own heart attack. Rumors ran wild that Hayes would retire. Instead, he lost 25 pounds, and following months of recuperating, he was back on the sidelines coaching the Buckeyes.

In 1974, Ohio State started off the season winning its first eight games by a combined score of 360-75. Everything seemed to be on track for a run at a national title. Then on November 9 at Michigan State, the number one-ranked Buckeyes suffered the most controversial loss in school history. With Ohio State leading the Spartans 13-3 early in the fourth quarter, Michigan State rallied to take a 16-13 lead. Starting from its own 29-yard line, OSU began to march down the field. Ohio State fullback Champ Henson dove to within inches of the goal line with 29 seconds remaining. The Spartans were slow to get off the pile and back to the line of scrimmage. When the ball was finally snapped, it went through the legs of OSU quarterback Cornelius Greene, where it was picked up and taken in for an apparent touchdown by wingback Brian Baschnagel. One official ruled it a touchdown, but another said time had run out. Chaos broke out on the field. As Hayes ran out to protest, MSU fans celebrated wildly on the field.

With Big Ten commissioner Wayne Duke in attendance, both teams were sent to their respective locker rooms as officials tried to sort out the finish. It's estimated that nearly half of the 78,533 fans in attendance stayed nearly 45 minutes to wait for the officials to rule on the ending of the contest. Head official Gene Calhoun told Duke time had run out before

OPPOSITE: OSU running back Archie Griffin (45) explodes up the middle as Michigan linebacker Carl Russ (33) looks to stop him. (Brockway Sports Photos)

the Buckeyes had finished the play. The OSU touchdown would not count. It was a crushing defeat for Ohio State, who fell in the rankings, coupled with Michigan's win over Illinois.

In the days leading up to the battle between the two schools, Schembechler commented that both teams' kicking games would play an important role in the upcoming contest. How prophetic Bo's comment was. Both teams were evenly matched. Michigan was ranked third by the Associated Press while Ohio State was fourth. The Wolverines were ranked first nationally in rushing defense, second in scoring defense and third in total defense. Their offense was ranked seventh in total offense. Meanwhile, the Buckeyes led the country in both team punting and kickoff returns while averaging a Big Ten-best 496 yards per game offensively. Ohio State's offense featured running back Archie Griffin, who was shooting for his second straight rushing title, averaging 146 yards per game in seven league games.

The build-up to the 1974 showdown was at its highest level in Columbus since 1970. It was to be the Buckeyes' revenge game after playing to a 10-10 tie in Ann Arbor in 1973, ruining OSU's shot of a national championship. Scalpers were getting top dollar for tickets as another record crowd of 88,243 showed up to watch the season-ending showdown.

Michigan received the opening kickoff, and just four plays later, quarterback Dennis Franklin hit wingback Gil Chapman on a 42-yard scoring strike as the Wolverines jumped out to a 7-0 lead. The Buckeyes' situation deteriorated quickly as they fumbled on their first possession at the Michigan 26-yard line. The Wolverines again drove down the field. Ohio State's defense was finally able to stop

Michigan on a third-down attempt at the Buckeyes' 20-yard line. Wolverines kicker Mike Lantry then sent a 38-yard field goal between the uprights as Michigan built a 10-0 lead with 4:57 remaining in the first quarter.

With the wind at their backs in the second quarter, the Buckeyes were able to put together three drives into Michigan territory. Ohio State place kicker Tom Klaban booted field goals of 47, 25 and 43 yards to bring Ohio State to within a point of Michigan at the half, 10-9.

Early in the third quarter with the Buckeyes again driving to the north end of the field, Klaban kicked his fourth field goal of the afternoon from 45 yards out to give Ohio State its first lead of the day, 12-10. While those would be the final points in the contest, the drama was just beginning. Late in the third quarter, the Michigan defense had stopped the Ohio State offense deep in OSU territory. Punting from the back of the Ohio State end zone, sophomore Tom Skladany came through with one of the finest punts in school history, a 63-yarder. Skladany's excellent punt, coupled with Ray Griffin's outstanding coverage, sent Michigan back to its 30-yard line with only 57 seconds remaining.

Franklin hit receiver Jim Smith on 23-yard pass play down to OSU's 31. His second pass fell incomplete, but tailback Rob Lytle ran for 10 yards and a first down at Ohio State's 21-yard line. Lytle then ran up the middle for six more yards to the Buckeyes' 15-yard line. With 18 seconds remaining, Schembechler elected to go for the field goal and the win.

The tension was tremendous. All 88,243 fans were on their feet screaming and wondering if the Wolverines could pull out the victory. Kicking into the north end of the stadium, with a strong wind behind him, Lantry launched a 38-yard field goal that sailed to the uprights. The Michigan players thought the attempt was good, but the officials signaled that the ball had gone just barely left as Ohio State won, 12-10. The Ohio State players celebrated on the field. For Lantry, the pain of missing was incredible. He had missed one earlier in the game from 49 yards out.

After the game, Schembechler told the *Columbus Dispatch,* along with the other assembled media, "With the mistakes that we made and the circumstances in the ball game, you can't really blame the kid who kicked the ball. We should have had the game out of reach by then." Prior to the 2003 Ohio State-Michigan game, Schembechler reflected back on the 1974 contest by saying: "Most of the games that I was involved in were defensive battles, a kicking battle." Chuckling out loud, Schembechler went on to say: " I was on the treadmill yesterday and they were playing that 1974 game and we missed the damn field goal. I mean we played a helluva game, but so did they. We got the ball late in the game and we were right down there to win the game and missed the field goal. It was good if it were kicked here, but it was kicked in Columbus, so down there it wasn't good."

Despite the Buckeyes' victory over Michigan, no one knew whether or not Ohio State would go to the Rose Bowl for a third straight year. The Big Ten athletic directors had to fly to Chicago the following day to vote on which team would represent the conference in Pasadena. Hayes told the *Columbus Dispatch* after the game: "I just don't think there's any question which team should go, but they'll have to vote. We beat the team we're tied with for the title, so the logical assumption would be that we'll go."

Schembechler had correctly predicted before the game that the Ohio State-Michigan contest would come down to the kicking game, and it did. Lantry's attempt that floated just left of the goal post cost Michigan an undisputed Big Ten championship, a trip to the Rose Bowl and an undefeated season. Skladany's monster punt of 63 yards got the Buckeyes out of trouble late in the game while walk-on placekicker Tom Klaban booted a record four field goals in the biggest game of the season.

Klaban, a Czechoslovakian refugee who immigrated to Cincinnati at the age of 14, was awarded a full scholarship after the game and the game ball. Hayes told the *Columbus Dispatch* after the game: "We had the greatest kicking coach of all time in Ernie Godfrey, and it's tradition that's carried right on." As far as the efforts by Skladany, who averaged 45.2 yards for five punts, with Michigan returning them for only 13 yards, Hayes said: "Our punting game was superb. The coverage, which was led by freshman Ray Griffin who had two great tackles, didn't allow them the kind of returns they've been getting, so we kept them sort of bottled up."

Offensively, Griffin rushed 25 times for 111 yards and would go on the following month to win the first of two straight Heisman Trophies presented annually to the nation's top collegiate player. Griffin, now in charge of the Ohio State Alumni Association, said: "The four field goals kicked by Klaban were truly outstanding. That was a very, very hard-fought football game. What I remember about it was that week of the game, one of the Michigan players had made a quote that 'If Archie Griffin gained over 100 yards, it would be over his dead body,' that was more than enough material for our team. Our offensive line took it personally. We went out there and I got over 100 yards in a hard-fought game. I had two hip pointers, our defense played hard, we got that ball in position, and Klaban did what he would normally do and that's come through. That game made everybody really,

really, really proud of Tom Klaban. He did a terrific job in that game. With the pressure on, he nailed them."

Statistically, the offensive numbers were virtually the same for both teams. Ohio State and Michigan both rushed for 195 yards with the Wolverines gaining 96 yards through the air compared to the Buckeyes' 56 yards passing. Franklin was picked off two times while Ohio State coughed the ball up twice on fumbles. Hayes was asked if the pressure got to him. Hayes would later tell the *Columbus Dispatch:* "If you get as much fun out of football as I do, enough to come back after a heart attack and go through this game without having another one, then I'd say I'm a tough old cuss."

Unfortunately for Ohio State, the Buckeyes lost the 1975 Rose Bowl to USC by a final of 18-17. The 10-2 Buckeyes finished fourth in the final Associated Press poll behind eventual national champion Oklahoma. USC was second with Michigan third. The Buckeyes outscored their 12 opponents 437-129, while scoring 59 touchdowns and putting up 5,252 total yards of offense. The two losses (Michigan State and USC) are hard to take for former members of the team, but the victory over Michigan would rank as one of the top 25 games of all time as the "Ten-Year War" between Hayes and Schembechler began to reach its zenith.

SCORES BY QUARTER	1ST	2ND	3RD	4TH	TOTAL
Michigan	10	0	0	0	10
Ohio State	0	9	3	0	12

1st Q-(UM) Franklin to Chapman 42-yd TD pass (7-0 UM)
1st Q-(UM) Lantry 38-yd FG (10-0 UM)
2nd Q-(OSU) Klaban 47-yd FG (10-3 UM)
2nd Q-(OSU) Klaban 25-yd FG (10-6 UM)
2nd Q-(OSU) Klaban 43-yd FG (10-9 UM)
3rd Q-(OSU) Klaban 45-yd FG (12-10 OSU)

1980 ROSE BOWL

USC 17, OHIO STATE 16

Each weekday between 12:00-1:00 p.m., I cohost a radio show called *Spielman on Sports* on Sports Radio 1460 "The Fan," WBNS-AM, in Columbus. As you can guess, the host of this fine program is legendary former Ohio State All-America linebacker and Lombardi Award winner Chris Spielman. In the past, I've been known to welcome a head coach or player by saying: "Congratulations on a great season!" Chris will immediately jump in and say: "Coach, as we all know, it wasn't a great season because you didn't reach your goal, and that of course is winning the championship." I always felt until recently that I was trying to be polite. But deep down, the player or coach knows Spiels is right. If you didn't win it all, your goal wasn't reached and that person will always be wondering, "what if?" What if I had made the catch for the winning touchdown, kicked a field goal with one second left on the clock, made the game-saving tackle or called the right play? Every player on every team that doesn't win its respective championship probably thinks about that from time to time. A victory in the 1980 Rose Bowl would complete a national championship season, while a loss would put Ohio State in the "what if" category.

The 1979 Buckeyes, under first-year head coach Earle Bruce, looked to be a team of destiny. No one could have predicted the success that awaited Ohio State following the dismal conclusion to the 1978 season. That season ended not only with a loss to Clemson in the Gator Bowl, but legendary head coach Woody

Hayes getting fired after punching Tigers linebacker Charlie Bauman on the OSU sideline.

Ohio State ran the table in 1979, going a perfect 11-0 while winning an outright Big Ten championship. A victory over Pac-10 champion USC, 10-0-1, in the 1980 Rose Bowl would give Ohio State its first national title since the super sophomores won it all in 1968. Ohio State had its chances to win other national titles in the 11 seasons that had passed, but always found a way to let them slip away. A loss at Michigan in 1969 along with Rose Bowl losses in 1971 and 1976 cost OSU three national titles. A 10-10 tie at Michigan in 1973 ruined yet another title opportunity.

Three days after the win at Michigan, the Buckeyes got a scare. On Tuesday, December 18, 1979, Coach Bruce was admitted to Riverside Hospital's coronary care unit for observation with chest pains. OSU team physician Dr. Bob Murphy later told reporters Bruce was suffering from a severe chest cold, but felt he should be placed under observation for 48 hours to monitor his condition. Assistant coaches Glen Mason and Dennis Fryzel temporarily ran the team's first two practices while Bruce recovered. The following Monday, the team, including Bruce, flew to Pasadena, California, as workouts for the 1980 Rose Bowl officially got underway.

Just as his predecessor Woody Hayes had done, Bruce kept the Buckeyes' practice sessions closed to the media. When they were not practicing, the OSU players had a chance to unwind by making the traditional visits to

ABOVE: USC tailback Charles White begins to cut to his left as OSU safety Todd Bell (25) closes in for the tackle. OSU's Bob Murphy (28) is also pictured. (Brockway Sports Photos)

Disneyland and Universal Studios. Unlike Hayes, Bruce allowed his players to fill up at Lawry's Prime Rib Restaurant in Beverly Hills. Ohio State's Tom Levenick, Mark Sullivan and Ron Barwing put on an eating performance for the ages. Levenick became the all-time Rose Bowl beef-eating champ by putting away 10 1/2 pounds of beef and was on his 11th prime rib when Bruce put an end to the gluttony. Bruce later told the *Columbus Dispatch's* Bob Hunter: "I don't like to promote that stuff. I'm going to take a look at those three guys in practice today and see how they do, I'll tell you that."

The Associated Press poll had Ohio State ranked first with USC second. In the UPI poll, USC was second with OSU ranked third. Ohio State's defense would have its hands full with running back Charles White, the Heisman Trophy winner (180.3 yards per game, 18 touchdowns), and USC's famous "student body right" formation. While at USC, White had rushed for 5,998 yards, the second highest in NCAA history. USC's huge offensive line received a boost before the Rose Bowl as left tackle Anthony Munoz announced that he would be ready to play after missing ten games due to a knee injury

At quarterback, the Trojans were led by Paul McDonald, who ranked third nationally in passing. He set a USC record with 143 passes without an interception while connecting on 64 percent of his passes for nearly 2,000 yards and 17 touchdowns. USC would face a Buckeye defense that ranked eighth nationally against scoring, allowing nearly 10 points per game.

Defensively, USC had given up 155 points on the season led by linebackers Chip Banks and Dennis Johnson along with deep backs Ronnie Lott and Dennis Smith. In Pac-10 games, the Trojans were ranked first against the run, fifth against the pass. Ohio State would counter offensively with running back

Calvin Murray, quarterback Art Schlichter and receivers Doug Donley and Gary Williams.

While the Big Ten conference had dominated the old Pac-8, now the Pac-10, between 1947 and 1969, the tide had turned against the teams from the Midwest. Since 1970, the Pac-10 had won nine of the past ten Rose Bowls with Michigan having lost five times, while OSU had lost four times. The pressure was on Ohio State to bring back a winner. USC entered the 1980 Rose Bowl with the best record in bowl history at 19-6, 16 of those victories coming in Pasadena. The Trojans had dominated the Rose Bowl in the 1970s, going 6-1 over the last seven years. Big Ten commissioner Wayne Duke told *The Los Angeles Times*: "I don't think the outcome of one bowl game necessarily reflects all the things that happened in a college football season. Just because we've lost these games, it isn't the death knell for Big Ten football."

Oddsmakers installed USC as a seven and a half-point favorite over the Buckeyes. Sportswriters were calling the Trojans "the team of the decade," despite the fact that they stood at 10-0-1. The only blemish was a 21-21 tie with Stanford. The Trojans rode into the Rose Bowl on a 19-game unbeaten streak and going back 26 games, stood 26-1-1. This was USC's 10th Rose Bowl appearance in the past 14 seasons.

On January 1, 1980, 105,526 fans were on hand to watch USC wage war on Ohio State. USC was able to move the ball early and jumped out to a 3-0 lead over Ohio State. Late in the first quarter, the Buckeyes' sputtering offense finally got things going as quarterback Art Schlichter hit receiver Gary Williams on a 67-yard strike down to the USC two-yard line. The Trojans, not known for their defense held OSU out of the end zone on four attempts. This would prove to be fatal later in the contest.

On the Buckeyes' next possession, Schlichter was on the move again with a 25-yard pass to Ty Hicks, down to the USC 33-yard line. But Hicks fumbled as he was going down, and the Trojans recovered the ball. McDonald then put together a five-play, 67-yard drive, finding receiver Kevin Williams on a 53-yard touchdown pass, giving the Trojans a 10-0 lead.

In the second quarter, Ohio State finally found the magic that had eluded them. Schlichter hit receiver Doug Donley on passes of 25 and 13 yards as the Buckeyes put together an 80-yard drive. This resulted in a Vlade Janakievski 35-yard field goal, pulling OSU to within seven points at 10-3.

Right before the half, safety Todd Bell knocked the ball away from White's arm, tackling him from behind. With the OSU offense back on the field, Schlichter fired a 67-yard touchdown bomb to Williams. Janakieski's extra point was good, and the game was tied at 10-all.

In the third quarter, Ohio State's offense picked up right where it had left off before halftime as Janakieski booted a 37-yard field goal. It gave OSU its first lead of the day at 13-10. As the momentum was building offensively, OSU's defense was having a tough time keeping White under control. He continued to pick up punishing yardage. USC was then called for offensive pass interference in the end zone, resulting in a touchback. This gave the Buckeyes control of the ball at their 20-yard line. Schlichter responded with another bomb, this one to Doug Donley for 58 yards early in the fourth quarter. Again, USC's defense held as Janakieski nailed a 24-yard field goal, his third of the day. It was a Rose Bowl record, giving OSU a 16-10 lead.

Late in the fourth quarter, USC put it all together in championship form. With the game on the line, the Trojans managed to streak down the field with a six-play, 83-yard drive, culminating in a one-yard touchdown run by White. Eric Hipp's conversion was good as the Trojans took a 17-16 lead over Ohio State with 1:32 remaining in the game. White showed why he was the nation's top running back, ripping off runs of 32 and 28 yards in what would prove to be the game-winning drive by USC.

Schlichter tried to lead a comeback Ohio State victory in the closing moments, but four of his passes in the final two minutes were incomplete. Ohio State suffered its third straight Rose Bowl defeat. It was the first loss in a magical season under Bruce.

Some 24 years later, Bruce stated what it's like to coach in the capital city: "Columbus has always been good to me. I've had a really good run in Columbus. I started as a student at Ohio State, I made a lot of friends, and I made a lot of friends as an assistant coach for six years under Coach Hayes. I made a lot of friends in nine years as the head football coach at Ohio State. No one can take that away from me! I love Columbus; I always have. I love the fans, I understand them and I understand that when you win you're great and when you lose you're terrible. I wouldn't have it any other way. You understand? I think that's what football fans should be, demanding. If you can't answer their questions, take the heat, then get the hell out of the profession!"

SCORES BY QUARTERS	1ST	2ND	3RD	4TH	TOTAL
USC	3	7	0	7	17
Ohio State	0	10	3	3	16

1st Q-(USC) Hipp 41-yd FG (3-0 USC)
2nd Q-(USC) McDonald 53-yd TD pass (10-0 USC)
2nd Q-(OSU) Janakievski 35-yd FG (10-3 USC)
2nd Q-(OSU) Schlichter to Murray, 67-yd TD pass (10-10)
3rd Q-(OSU) Janakievski 37-yd FG (13-10 OSU)
4th Q-(OSU) Janakievski 24-yd FG (16-10 OSU)
4th Q-(USC) White 1-yd TD (17-16 USC)

1998

MICHIGAN STATE 28, OHIO STATE 24

It may be wrong to categorize this game as one of the greatest in Ohio State football history, but it is one of the most important games in the heights and depths of Buckeye lore. The easiest thing I could have done is to write only about the great victories. There have been some momentous wins that I could have placed in this book and didn't. To truly understand and fully appreciate an important victory, teams and their fans have to have suffered the heartache of a painful loss or losses. Each team, no matter how successful, has endured a loss that shouldn't have happened. Years later, coaches, players and fans shake their heads at "the one that got away" and ruined a dream season.

Coming off a 10-3 season in 1997, expectations were high that the Ohio State Buckeyes might have the right ingredients for a run at the national title in 1998. Four of the five starting offensive linemen from the previous season were back to anchor a line that would protect quarterback Joe Germaine, the hero of the 1997 Rose Bowl. The hated two-quarterback system was a thing of the past with Stan Jackson's graduation. Germaine now had the position all to himself and looked forward to showing what he could do in a full-time role throwing to the likes of David Boston at split end, Dee Miller at the flanker position and big John Lumpkin at tight end. Michael Wiley started at tailback, while Matt Keller returned as the fullback.

Defensively, the Ohio State secondary and linebacking corps were outstanding. Andy Katzenmoyer anchored the middle linebacking position while Jerry Rudzinski and Na'il Diggs handled the outside positions. The secondary was deep and talented. Antoine Winfield and Ahmed Plummer were two of the best cornerbacks in OSU history with Damon Moore and Gary Berry working as the safeties. Dan Stultz returned as the place-kicker with long-range bomber Brent Bartholomew handling the punting duties.

Ohio State head coach John Cooper entered his 11th season at the helm of the Buckeyes and knew that he might have the right ingredients to win it all in 1998. The Buckeyes had come so close in recent years to capturing that elusive national championship, only to lose their first game of the season in 1993, 1995 and 1996 in the final game to Michigan. Despite OSU's recent successes, the wolves were at Cooper's door. His record against Michigan stood at 1-8-1, which included a three-game losing streak to the Wolverines. Fans were growing restless and not only wanted a victory over Michigan, but a chance to play for the national title as well.

The 1998 season started off on a strong note for the Buckeyes as Ohio State won their September 5 opener on the road at West Virginia, 34-17. The Buckeyes then beat Toledo and Missouri to wrap up nonconference play at 3-0. On October 3, Ohio State

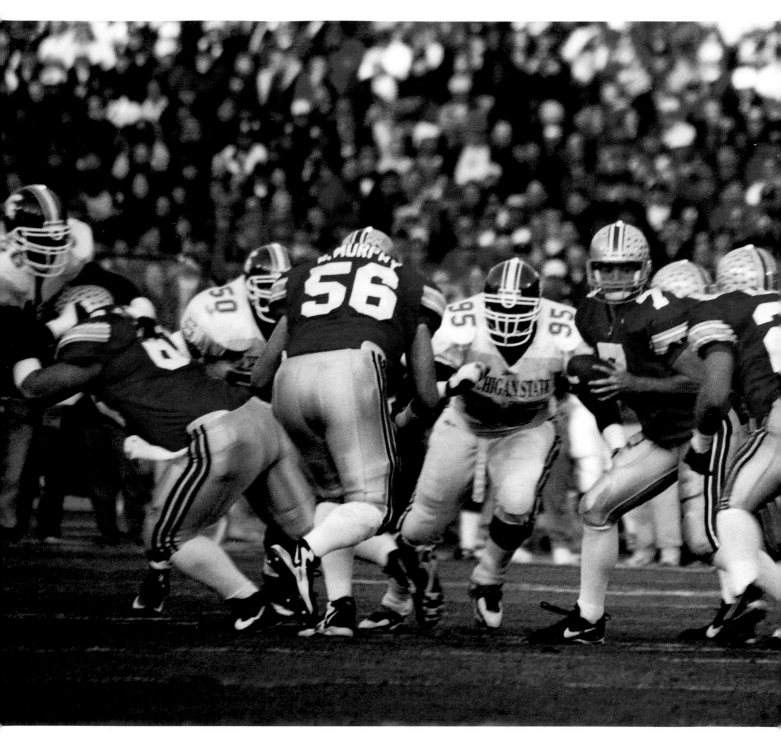

ABOVE: OSU quarterback Joe Germaine looks to hand the ball off to fullback Matt Keller as left guard Rob Murphy (56) prepares to open up a hole. (Brockway Sports Photos)

opened their Big Ten schedule by winning convincingly over Penn State 28-9 before crushing Illinois on the road, 41-0. The Buckeyes then returned to Ohio Stadium for homecoming and beat up Minnesota, 45-14. Ohio State then followed that up with road victories at Northwestern (36-10) and Indiana (38-7).

Everything seemed to be going Ohio State's way. The team had dominated every team they had played and stood at a perfect 8-0 on the season. The Bowl Championship Series poll had been released prior to the victory at Indiana. Ohio State checked in ranked second. Following the win over the Hoosiers, the Buckeyes had moved up to number one in the BCS with Tennessee second. UCLA had been second in the BCS, but fell to third after a close win over Stanford. Germaine told the *Columbus Dispatch:* "That just goes to show any given week you can be challenged by anybody. I guess Stanford was a 1-6 team and they played UCLA down to the last play. So you've got to keep your heads on." The top two teams in the final BCS ratings on December 6 would play for the national title in the Fiesta Bowl on January 4, 1999.

Number one-ranked Ohio State entered their November 7 home showdown against Michigan State as a heavy favorite. The Buckeyes were 8-0 on the season and favored by 27 and a half points over 4-4 Michigan State. The Buckeyes had dominated every team that they had played, while MSU was a "Jekyll-and-Hyde" team. The Spartans had crushed Notre Dame 45-23 while being demolished by Oregon (48-14) and Michigan (29-17). The Spartans players were outspoken heading into the contest. The *Columbus Dispatch* quoted MSU defensive end Robaire Smith as saying: "Everybody is expecting us to go in there and just try to keep the score close. But we expect to win. Everybody says we should try to upset them. I feel they've got to try to upset us. We're a good team. We've had some ups and downs, but we ain't some pushover."

At 8-0 on the season, the Ohio State offense was in top form. Germaine had passed for over 2,200 yards and 17 touchdowns while only tossing four interceptions. The stoic leader had topped 300 yards passing five times in 1998, including the last four games, both OSU records. The Buckeyes led the Big Ten in total yards (512.1 average) and were second in passing (302.6) and in rushing (209.5) per game.

Defensively, Ohio State entered the contest third nationally while leading the Big Ten in total defense (237.4 average). With their outstanding secondary, OSU was number one in pass defense efficiency, fifth against the run (83.5 yard average) and ranked third in scoring defense (9.0 point average). If there was any foreboding heading into the contest, Plummer told Tim May of the *Columbus Dispatch:* "A lot of times college football is really about matchups. Different teams match up better against some teams than others. They [Spartans] might have just had a better matchup against Michigan or whoever they played before or after the game." As good as both Plummer and Winfield were in the defensive secondary, the coaches were concerned about stopping Spartans receiver Plaxico Burress. The lanky 6'5" receiver would have a huge advantage over either Plummer or Winfield, who stood at 5' 9".

On November 7, 1998, number-one Ohio State (8-0) hosted the Michigan State Spartans (4-4) in a late afternoon game at Ohio Stadium. The game looked to be a blowout early on in the first quarter as OSU scored 17 points. The Buckeyes took the opening kickoff and raced 72 yards before MSU's defense held on third down near their goal line. Ohio State kicker Dan Stultz booted a 20-yard field goal, and the Buckeyes led, 3-0.

Michigan State answered with an 11-play, 60-yard drive that resulted in a Paul Edinger 33-yard field goal to tie the game at 3-3. The quick-scoring Buckeyes marched right back down the field with a five-play, 80-yard touchdown drive, culminating in a 41-yard touchdown pass to tight end John Lumpkin. Stultz's extra point was good and OSU led, 10-3. Later in the first quarter, Ohio State tailback Michael Wiley scored from one yard out, and the Buckeyes' lead increased to 17-3 following another Stultz extra point.

The Ohio State offense cooled off in the second quarter as Michigan State's defense began to take control, keeping OSU from adding to their point total. The Spartans managed two more field goals to tighten the score, before halftime, at 17-9.

In the third quarter, Moore picked off a Burke pass and raced 73 yards for a touchdown. Stultz added the extra point as Ohio State took a commanding 24-9 lead with 9:51 left in the third. Then the turning point in the game happened after OSU's defense stopped Michigan State. The Spartans' Craig Jarrett punted the ball, which went off the back of freshman Nate Clements. Michigan State's Scott Erneberger recovered at the Spartans' own 49-yard line. With new life, MSU's offense came back onto the field. Facing a third and eight from OSU's 49-yard line, Burke found Scott on a 28-yard pass play. Two plays later, Burke connected with Lavalle Richardson on a 23-yard touchdown strike.

The Spartans failed on their two-point conversion as the Ohio State lead remained at 24-15.

Michigan State then recovered an Ohio State fumble (one of four on the day) as the pendulum continued to swing in the Spartans favor. Four plays later, Edinger booted a career-long 49-yard field goal to cut the OSU lead down to 24-18. Late in the third quarter, Michigan State put together an eight-play, 92-yard scoring drive as running back Sedrick Irvin plunged in from three yards out for a touchdown. Edinger's extra point was good as the Spartans grabbed their first lead of the day at 25-24 with 14:20 left in the fourth quarter. Then, following another OSU turnover, Edinger booted his school record-tying fifth field goal of the afternoon from 42 yards out as MSU increased their lead to 28-24 with 9:26 left on the clock.

The stunned crowd at Ohio Stadium could hardly believe their eyes. What once seemed to be an inevitable blowout early on by the Buckeyes had changed into a possible defeat by a .500 team. How could this be? The answer was turnovers. Ohio State had fumbled the ball four times in the afternoon, allowing Michigan State back into the game. Any coach will tell you that turnovers are a great equalizer in a game. Once a team gets a few breaks, their confidence begins to soar while the other team begins to doubt themselves.

Following Michigan State's ensuing kickoff, Ohio State's offense went back onto the field and put together an all-run drive down to MSU's 26. There, facing a fourth and one, the Spartans stuffed OSU backup tailback Joe Montgomery for no gain. After stopping the Spartans' next offensive series, David Boston returned a Michigan State punt 27 yards to the Ohio State 49-yard line. Everyone was confident in the Ohio State huddle. The Buckeyes' offense seemed to be coming around, they were playing in front of their fans, and it was crunch time. With only 1:39 left in the fourth quarter, Germaine led the Buckeyes on their final drive of the game. The fifth-year senior quarterback connected with Boston on a 16-yard completion before finding tight end John Lumpkin for 20 more yards down to the MSU 15. Anticipation was high that the Buckeyes would score a touchdown to win the game, stay undefeated, and keep their dreams alive for OSU's first national championship since 1968 while also retaining their number-one ranking in the BCS.

On first down, Germaine attempted a lob pass to Boston, but it was tipped away by Cedric Henry. Germaine then tossed the ball away on second down trying to avoid heavy pressure by the Spartans. Michigan State defensive back Renaldo Hill broke up a sharply thrown third-down pass to Dee Miller at the goal line. Now, facing fourth down, Germaine dropped back to pass, only to have Hill intercept the ball at the goal line to seal Michigan State's improbable victory, 28-24, over top-ranked Ohio State in Ohio Stadium. The Spartans, who had ruined Ohio State's chances for a national championship by beating the Buckeyes in 1972 and '74, had done so again in 1998.

Afterwards, Spartans head coach Nick Saban, who would later coach LSU to the 2004 national championship, a former Ohio State assistant coach (1980-81) told the *Columbus Dispatch:* "I remember in 1981 when I was on the staff here, we went up to Michigan as 10-point underdogs and they had been ranked number one at some point in that season. Coach [Woody] Hayes gave a really

inspiring talk to the team, and one thing he told the players was, 'You can have no great wins unless there's tremendous adversity.' We played as well as we could play. We were a little bit outmatched, but we won that game."

In the Ohio State locker room, Cooper told the *Columbus Dispatch:* "Give them credit. They outcoached us, they outplayed us, their defense was better than ours, their kicking game was better than ours and of course, they came away with the victory." With the loss, Ohio State dropped to 8-1 overall, 5-1 in the Big Ten. MSU improved to 5-4 overall and 3-2 in the conference. The Buckeyes would go on to win at Iowa the following week (45-14) before clobbering Michigan 31-16 at Ohio Stadium. Ohio State then finished up their season on New Year's Day with a convincing 24-14 victory over Texas A&M in the Sugar Bowl. The 11-1 Buckeyes outscored their opponents 430-144 while capturing a Big Ten co-championship along with winning the Sugar Bowl. The quest to become national champions would end four years later, with a new coach.

SCORES BY QUARTERS	1ST	2ND	3RD	4TH	TOTAL
Michigan State	3	6	9	10	28
Ohio State	17	0	7	0	24

1st Q-(OSU) Stultz 20-yd FG (3-0 OSU)
1st Q-(MSU) Edinger 33-yd FG (3-3)
1st Q-(OSU) Germaine to Lumpkin 41-yd TD (10-3 OSU)
1st Q-(OSU) Wiley 1-yd TD (17-3 OSU)
2nd Q-(MSU) Edinger 43-yd FG (17-6 OSU)
2nd Q-(MSU) Edinger 22-yd FG (17-9 OSU)
3rd Q-(OSU) Moore 73-yd interception return for a TD (24-9 OSU)
3rd Q-(MSU) Burke to L. Richardson 23-yd TD (Ex. Point failed 24-15 OSU)
3rd Q-(MSU) Edinger 49-yd FG (24-18 OSU)
4th Q-(MSU) Irvin 3-yd TD (25-24 MSU)
4th Q-(MSU) Edinger 42-yd FG (28-24 MSU)

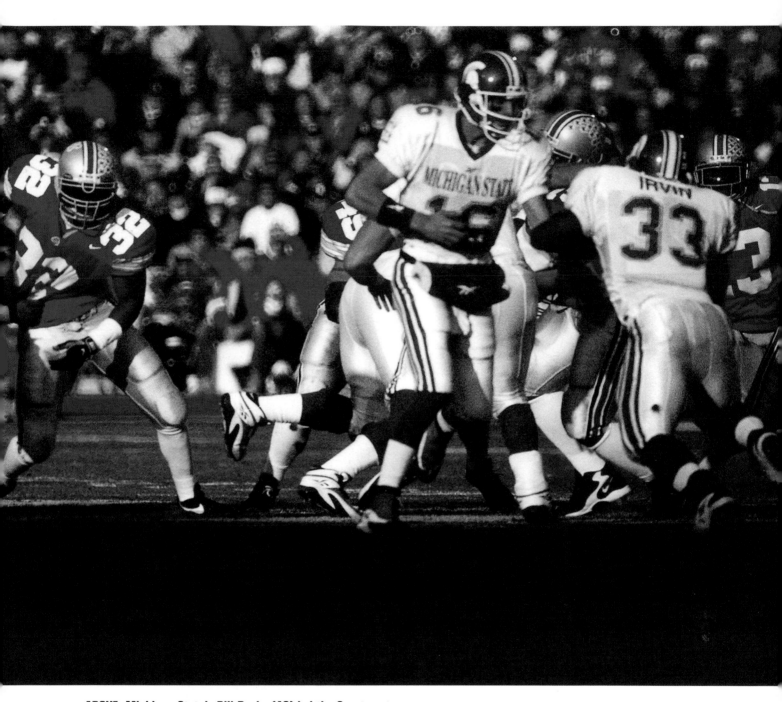

ABOVE: Michigan State's Bill Burke (16) led the Spartans to a stunning upset of Ohio State. (Brockway Sports Photos)

1957

Ohio State 17, Iowa 13

For some reason, when fans think of the great football teams in Ohio State history, the 1957 squad seems to go under the radar. Perhaps it's because they lost their first game of the season to Texas Christian University and didn't finish up with a perfect record. It might also have to do with a 10-7 win in the 1958 Rose Bowl, a game that didn't impress the public. Either way, it's a team that deserves respect among the greats in OSU history.

Following its September 28 season opening loss at home to TCU, Ohio State managed to roll off consecutive victories over Washington, Illinois, Indiana, Wisconsin, Northwestern and Purdue. At 6-1 (5-0) in Big Ten play, Ohio State seemed to go back to its old ways and had moved up to sixth place in the AP and UPI weekly polls.

On November 16, 1957, a record crowd of 82,935 packed Ohio Stadium as the Buckeyes welcomed in the fifth-ranked Iowa Hawkeyes. Iowa, who was also having a fine season (6-0-1), (5-0-1) following a 21-21 tie with Michigan two weeks prior, was listed as a six-point favorite heading into the contest. The winner would automatically win the Big

Ten Championship and engraved invitation to the Rose Bowl. If that was not enough incentive, OSU owed Iowa, who snapped the Buckeyes' 17-game Big Ten winning streak the year before in Iowa City, 6-0.

With head coach Woody Hayes's close friend, Vice President Richard Nixon, in attendance, Ohio State scored first on a Don Sutherin field goal to take an early 3-0 lead. Iowa struck back as quarterback Randy Duncan found end Bob Prescott on an eight-yard touchdown pass. The Hawkeyes' extra-point attempt failed and Iowa led, 6-3.

In the second quarter, behind the running of fullback Bob White, OSU regained the lead, driving 80 yards to score a touchdown. Quarterback Frank Kremblas sneaked it in from one yard out as the Buckeyes took a 10-6 lead into the half.

It was back and forth in the third quarter as Duncan concluded a 70-yard drive by scoring to give Iowa a 13-10 advantage. Iowa's run defense, ranked second nationally at 89 yards per game heading into the contest, was able to shut down the powerful OSU attack the rest of the third quarter and early fourth. Part of the reason was the injury of the Buckeyes'

OPPOSITE: Head coach Woody Hayes along with fullback Bob White donate their time for a local charity fundraising event. (Ohio State University Photo Archive)

leading rusher, halfback Don Clark. He was out because of a groin injury suffered the week before at Purdue. Clark, who led the Buckeyes in rushing, total offense, and scoring, spearheaded Ohio State's rushing attack offense which ranked sixth at nearly 288 yards per game.

Ohio State seemed to be ready to respond to Iowa's latest score on the next series. Following the ensuing kickoff, OSU uncharacteristically tried two straight passes that fell incomplete. On third and 10 from their own 25-yard line, Kremblas found Joe Cannavino for 16 yards and a first down at the Buckeyes' 41-yard line. White then broke through the center for 30 yards. Three plays later at the Iowa 16-yard line, OSU's drive was halted as Iowa intercepted Kremblas's pass and returned to the Hawkeyes' 22.

Neither team was able to do anything with the ball until midway through the fourth quarter when Ohio State took over at its own 32-yard line following an Iowa punt. With 7:51 left on the clock, the sold-out crowd at Ohio Stadium knew that the Buckeyes' chances to win a Big Ten title and a trip to the Rose Bowl might ride on this drive.

What happened next went down as one of the greatest achievements in Ohio State football history. White, a 215-pound redhead out of Covington, Kentucky, virtually took over the contest. Hayes's famous "Three yards and a cloud of dust offense," led by White and his offensive line, took the fight to the reigning Big Ten champions.

White first went over right tackle for four yards followed by nine yards and a first down after going over left guard. With first and 10 at the OSU 45-yard line, White then broke through over right guard for 29 yards and a first down at Iowa's 26-yard line. With the game's momentum swinging to the Buckeyes,

Ohio State was daring one of the best defenses in the country to stop a no-frills offense of power football.

Following his 29-yard run, Hayes opted to give White a breather and gave the ball to London, Ohio native, junior halfback Dick LeBeau, who went over right guard for three yards. With the crowd yelling "Give it to White," Kremblas handed off to White who powered his way up the middle for five yards followed by ten more and a first down at Iowa's eight-yard line. With the entire stadium on its feet, White went over the middle again for three yards, setting up one of the biggest scores in OSU history, a five-yard touchdown run over the left side to give the Buckeyes the winning score. Sutherin's extra point was good as the Buckeyes took a 17-13 lead. White had carried the ball on seven of eight carries for 65 of the 68 yards. White ended up with 157 yards and a touchdown on 22 carries.

On the next series, OSU senior guard Bill Jobko intercepted a Duncan pass on the Buckeyes' 32. Ohio State then went three and out, punting the ball down to Iowa's 31-yard line. With just 36 seconds remaining, Duncan threw three incomplete passes as the Buckeyes held on for not only their greatest victory of the season, but of all time. So tremendous was the victory that the crowd rushed the field, broke down and uprooted the concrete-anchored goal posts. Most of the crowd stayed to soak in what they had witnessed on the field and listen to the band perform their postgame celebration.

The 17-13 win was Ohio State's sixth consecutive Big Ten victory of the season and its 23rd in the last 25th starts. What made the win even sweeter was the fact that it was done without their leading ground gainer and All-America halfback candidate Don Clark, who was out with an injury. In fact, OSU took a big step towards beating Iowa back on Monday. Sensing the Buckeyes was "down" following Clark's injury, Hayes told his team that they would win, "with or without Clark." A bold statement heading into the biggest game of the year against the '56 Big Ten champs. No one could have predicted that White would have the impact that he did in the game. It was due to Clark's injury that White received his chance. Not at halfback like Clark, but at fullback.

White had played in a few relief chores at fullback in the TCU, Washington and Illinois games before being switched over to offensive center. He then served time as offensive and defensive center and offensive fullback in a limited role along with defensive fullback. He played a larger role in the win over Wisconsin when he recovered a midair fumble in Ohio State's 16-13 win over Wisconsin. It wasn't until the Iowa game that White shone, carrying the ball 22 times for 157 yards and a touchdown. All of this against a massive Iowa defensive line led by All-American Alex Karras and 251-pound Dick Klein, who were giving up a miniscule 2.2 yards per carry.

While White sat afterwards in the locker room reflecting on what had happened in the win over Iowa, bedlam broke out. Before there was the traditional Gatorade bath, where players on the sidelines dumped a cooler of drinks onto the head coach, the players shoved Coach Hayes under the showers, drenching their victorious head coach in a wild celebration. Some 45 years later, LeBeau told WBNS-AM in Columbus: "It was one of the craziest parties I can ever remember in all of my high school, OSU and NFL days. It was a whole lot of fun."

Before Hayes was carried to the showers, he, along with assistant coach Ernie Godfrey,

stood crying over the emotional victory. According to accounts in the *Columbus Dispatch,* Godfrey said: "This was the greatest coaching triumph I've seen in 39 years…and I'm not taking anything away from the other coaches when I say that."

The great Chick Harley was in the locker room as well, and the players cheered for him. Woody held up his hand as Harley said, "I thought it would be a great game, and I was right." Harley hesitated, and Woody helped him out by saying, "and the right team won, didn't it, Chick?" Harley said, "That's right. The right team won," as the players cheered again.

Later, Hayes was handed a piece of paper with quotations from Iowa head coach Forest Evashevski: "Iowa made too many mistakes to win. Ohio played smarter and harder football, and they deserved to win. I want to congratulate the new champion. I know Ohio State will wear the crown well and that the Buckeyes will do a fine job of representing the Big Ten in the Rose Bowl." After reading the statement out loud, Hayes put down the sheet and said: "That was darn nice of him. This Iowa team is explosive. It was a rock-'em, sock-'em game and we were just that much better than they were." In saying this, Hayes put his thumb and forefinger nearly together, with just a bit of light showing in between to emphasize his statement.

The victory over Iowa gave the Buckeyes the 1957 Big Ten title. It was the first time in history Ohio State had wrapped up the championship as early as the eighth game of the season with one game to play, at Michigan. It was the ninth undisputed championship and eleventh overall, which included two co-championships. Former OSU defensive lineman Jim Marshall, who would later play in four Super Bowls with the Minnesota Vikings, told WBNS-AM: "It was a wonderful season.

"It was a wonderful season. I like to say that we were riding the crest of the wave. It was the best of times, especially when you're winning and Woody Hayes is your coach. It's a good, good thing."

—OSU defensive lineman Jim Marshall

I like to say that we were riding the crest of the wave. It was the best of times, especially when you're winning and Woody Hayes is your coach. It's a good, good thing."

Hayes's teams had now tied Minnesota's powerhouse teams of the mid-30s with three conference championships in four years. Bernie Bierman's Gopher squads did it in 1934-35-37, winning 15 and losing none. The Buckeyes won 19 in the Big Ten in 1954-55-57 with a chance to make it 20 the following Saturday with a win at Michigan. For his seven years at Ohio State, Hayes owned a 46-15-2 record. The following week, Ohio State trounced Michigan in Ann Arbor, 31-14, to finish up at 8-1 overall, 7-0 in the conference. A neat nugget for trivia buffs: OSU guard Bill Jobko is the only player in Big Ten history to play on three undisputed league champions.

OSU would go on to beat Oregon in a lackluster Rose Bowl 10-7 to capture the UPI 1957 national championship.

While it's easy for fans to remember the more recent championships, the 1957 season had everything but a perfect record. A decisive win at Michigan along with a victory in the 1958 Rose Bowl over Oregon would follow.

SCORES BY QUARTER	1ST	2ND	3RD	4TH	TOTAL
Iowa	6	0	7	0	13
Ohio State	3	7	0	7	17

1st Q-(OSU) Sutherin 18-yd FG (3-0 OSU)
1st Q-(IOWA) Duncan to Prescott 8-yd TD (Extra Point Failed, 6-3 Iowa)
2nd Q-(OSU) Kremblas 1-yd TD (10-6 OSU)
3rd Q-(IOWA) Duncan 1-yd TD (13-10 Iowa)
4th Q-(OSU) White 5-yd TD (17-13 OSU)

ABOVE: Bob White had one of his finest games against Iowa, rushing for 157 yards. (Ohio State University Photo Archive)

1975

OHIO STATE 21, MICHIGAN 14

One of the greatest games in Ohio State football history occurred on November 22, 1975, in Ann Arbor against the Michigan Wolverines. The winner, as had become the norm over the past seven seasons, would represent the Big Ten conference in the Rose Bowl while the loser, for a change, didn't get left out of postseason action.

Following Michigan's 12-10 loss in Columbus the previous November, Wolverines head coach Bo Schembechler argued the conference athletic directors should vote to allow Big Ten schools, other than the Rose Bowl representative, to participate in other Bowl games if so invited. Schembechler argued that his Michigan teams had gone 30-2-1 over the last three seasons only to have Ohio State nudge them out of a Rose Bowl appearance with two wins and a tie. According to the Associated Press, following the 1974 loss to Ohio State, Schembechler stated at his weekly press conference: "It's a shame people can't see Michigan play in a bowl game. Michigan has the greatest defensive football team in the nation, bar none. I'm not saying that we should be in the Rose Bowl. That was lost on the football field, but we should be allowed to play in another bowl."

Ohio State had been sitting pretty in the catbird seat, having gone to the Rose Bowl the past three seasons. But Michigan was stewing over the matter of producing great teams that had to watch the bowl action from home. Out on the West Coast, resentment was building

towards USC, which had represented the Pac-8 conference in the Rose Bowl five of the last seven years, with Stanford having gone in 1971-72. The Big Ten's athletic directors approved the change, which was then ratified by the conference faculty council members. The Pac-8 conference, which had written the original paperwork for the Rose Bowl agreement, signed off on the deal as well. The Big Ten would now allow its top two teams to play in the Rose and Orange Bowls on New Year's Day starting in 1976.

While the winner of the 1975 Ohio State-Michigan grudge match would represent the conference in the Rose Bowl, the loser would receive an invitation to play in the Orange Bowl in Miami, Florida. For once, the loser wouldn't be left entirely out in the cold and could show the rest of the country the strength of the Big Ten conference.

Since the big upset victory over the Buckeyes in 1969, Michigan head coach Bo Schembechler had beaten OSU just once in the past five meetings. That one happened to be a 10-7 victory in 1971, against a Buckeye squad that finished the season by losing its final three games to end up at 6-4. After an 8-3 season in 1969, Schembechler's teams won an incredible .903 of their games from 1970 until prior to the 1975 contest against Ohio State. The only problem was, in his first six seasons, the Wolverines never won their final game of the year. Michigan lost the 1970 and 1972 Rose Bowls

ABOVE: OSU fullback Pete Johnson scores the winning touchdown as quarterback Cornelius Green (7) and running back Archie Griffin (45) celebrate. (Brockway Sports Photos)

while falling to OSU in 1972 and 1974. In 1973, the teams played to a 10-10 tie. Schembechler hoped to change his team's fortunes against the Buckeyes in 1975.

Heading into the matchup, both coaches played it close to the vest. Both closed down their practices to the media, extremely wary that team secrets might be stolen. According to the *Columbus Dispatch:* "It only takes one person who knows what he's looking for to ruin all of your preparations," said Hayes. After being spotted by Michigan's coaching staff, Ann Arbor police confiscated film from a news photographer. He was taking pictures of the Wolverines practicing from a third-floor apartment balcony with a telephoto lens. The photographer turned out to be a freelancer on assignment for United Press International.

As seemed to be happening on an annual basis, a record crowd of 105,543 fans crammed inside venerable Michigan Stadium to watch top-ranked Ohio State put its 10-0 record on the line against the 8-0-2 and fifth-ranked Wolverines. Both teams had 7-0 conference records. The winner would capture an outright Big Ten championship and a trip to the Rose Bowl. The loser would travel south to Miami to play in the Orange Bowl against the winner of the Big Eight title game between Oklahoma and Nebraska.

The first time Ohio State touched the ball, they drove 63 yards on 15 plays for a touchdown. Quarterback Cornelius Greene hit fullback Pete Johnson on a seven-yard pass with 4:43 left in the first quarter for the score. Tom Klaban's extra point was good as the Buckeyes made it 7-0.

Following an excellent opening drive by OSU, neither team could get on track, as Michigan lost both fumbles and freshman quarterback Rick Leach tossed an interception. Meanwhile, Ohio State followed up its touchdown with two interceptions and a lost fumble. Just when everybody was thinking they were watching Northwestern take on Indiana, Michigan put together an 80-yard scoring drive. Wolverines freshman quarterback Rick Leach looked like a four-year starter as he fired 42 yards' worth of passes to split end Keith Johnson while running back Gordon Bell broke up the passes with strong runs. With Michigan at Ohio State's 11-yard line, everyone was looking for Bell to run the ball. Instead, Bell took a pitch to the right side, stopped and fired a pass to wingback Jim Smith for the score. Bob Wood's extra point was good to even up the score at 7-7 just before halftime.

In the fourth quarter Michigan finally got a break. Following two failed runs, Ohio State punter Tom Skladany was brought in to punt on third down from his end zone and shanked one that went out at Ohio State's 43-yard line. Michigan then proceeded to put together its first scoring drive since late in the second quarter as Leach scored on a one-yard touchdown run with 7:11 remaining in the fourth quarter. Wood's extra point was good. The Wolverines' lead had grown to 14-7.

Michigan's defense had held Ohio State's powerful offense without a first down since early in the second quarter and were hoping they could do it one final time. Instead, the Buckeyes responded with one of their best drives of the season. On third and 10 from the OSU 20-yard line, wingback Brian Baschnagel came through with a 17-yard reception from his scrambling quarterback Corny Green. Baschnagel would later tell the *Columbus Dispatch* that an announcement over the Michigan Stadium loudspeakers fired him up: "They announced that Oklahoma was leading Nebraska, 7-3," he said, "and I said to myself, 'Hey, Michigan can win the national championship that we wanted so bad,' and that inspired me. I thought, 'This could be for

"I'd have to say this is our greatest comeback, so this has got to be the greatest game I've ever coached."

—Buckeyes coach Woody Hayes

everything.' After I saw Corny scramble, I just tried to get open, and I did."

With the momentum building like a locomotive leaving the station, the Ohio State offense had finally found its rhythm. Green then completed three passes that set up an 11-yard run by Archie Griffin. Green then ran 12 yards down to the eight-yard line for a first down. Then, three plays later, on fourth and goal, big Pete Johnson powered his way into the end zone for his second touchdown of the day. The extra point was good as Ohio State pulled even with the Wolverines at 14-14, with only 3:18 remaining in the game.

Michigan, knowing that a tie would send Ohio State to the Rose Bowl, was forced to start airing the ball down the field starting at its own 20-yard line. With the pressure on, Aaron Brown sacked Leach for a nine-yard loss. Second down brought an incomplete pass by Leach. Third down will live forever in the minds of those who witnessed Griffin, not Archie, but little brother Ray, picking off Leach's pass on Michigan's 32 and taking it back to the three-yard line. It was an extraordinary play by Griffin, whose coverage of a Tom Skladany punt the year before had helped out the Buckeyes in another crucial moment. On first down from the Michigan three-yard line, Pete Johnson bullied his way into the end zone for his third touchdown of

the day, and following the extra point, the Buckeyes led 21-14 with only 2:19 left in the contest. Ohio State, who couldn't make a first down for two and a half quarters, had now scored two touchdowns in a span of 59 seconds.

Now in desperation mode, Michigan's offense tried to become something they were not: a two-minute drill team. Facing a fourth and eight, Leach fired a pass OSU safety Craig Cassady picked off. For Cassady, son of the 1955 Heisman Trophy winning Howard "Hopalong" Cassady, it was his second interception of the day with only 1:15 remaining in the game. The Buckeyes ran out the last minute to win by a final of 21-14. For the first time since taking over the Wolverines back in 1969, coach Bo Schembechler had lost a conference game at Michigan Stadium. In fact, it was the Wolverines' first home loss in their last 41 games, an incredible defeat.

Afterward, 62-year-old Woody Hayes, whose record now stood at 16-8-1 against Michigan, told the *Columbus Dispatch:* "I'd have to say this is our greatest comeback, so this has got to be the greatest game I've ever coached."

As far as Archie Griffin's 31-game consecutive streak of 100-yard rushing performances coming to an end with just 46, Hayes replied: "I don't think that Arch is any more worried about that than I am," he said. "I've never seen a more unselfish team player. I've never seen one like him."

In 2004, Archie Griffin confirmed what Coach Hayes had said in the locker room some 29 years earlier by saying: "I was really proud of Ray that day. That was a hard-fought football game. For Ray to get that interception and to take it down to the three-yard line where big Pete Johnson took it home for the winning touchdown was terrific, for all of us. That interception was something really, really special, for me and for the rest of the seniors. That meant that we never lost to Michigan, having gone 3-0-1. To me, that was more important than getting 100 yards."

Before the 2003 Ohio State-Michigan contest, Ray Griffin looked back on the victory with pride: "It was probably the biggest play of my career at Ohio State. In fact, it's the most memorable play of my career, either in college or the pros. When we went into Michigan Stadium, they had not lost a home game in 41 straight home contests, and we had to go in there with our 'A game.' I look at football as a team sport, and we as a team stepped up that day. On that third-down play when Leach threw the interception deep, we were in a cover three and I was able to pick it off and take it down the sidelines to the three-yard line. Pete then scored, so it was a total team effort."

Ohio State headed to Pasadena, California, for a fourth straight season to play at the L.A. Coliseum. At that time both UCLA and USC played at the Coliseum. Their opponent was UCLA, a team they had beaten on October 4 by a final of 41-20 in the Los Angeles Coliseum. The Buckeyes, ranked number one in the country, lost a stunner to the heavy underdog Bruins, 23-10. The loss

dashed any hopes of OSU winning its first national championship since 1968 as they wound up at 11-1 on the season and fourth in the final AP poll behind national champion Oklahoma, Arizona State, and Alabama. UCLA finished fifth, behind Ohio State, with Michigan ranked sixth after losing in the Orange Bowl, 14-6, to Oklahoma. Jeff Logan, who would later replace Griffin as running back in 1976, played mainly with the special teams units in 1975 and laments the national title that slipped away: "We still have our Big Ten championship rings from that year with a band around the outside, which is empty. That band was supposed to say 'National Champions.' It was designed for the purpose of saying 'National Champions' on the outside, and it doesn't say that. I don't wear it today, not because of that reason, but every time I look at that game, it's beautiful, but there's something missing around the outside band."

The 1975 victory over Michigan remains to this day one of the greatest victories in Ohio State history, capping a four-year reign of terror over the Wolverines. In that four-year span, the Buckeyes went 40-5-1, including a 3-0-1 mark against the Wolverines. Ohio State won outright or shared four Big Ten titles while earning four straight Rose Bowl appearances. Archie Griffin finished his illustrious career at OSU by winning his second straight Heisman Trophy. Griffin and punter Tom Skladany repeated as All-Americans while offensive lineman Ted Smith and defensive back Tim Fox were named to the All-America squad for the first time. Quarterback Cornelius Greene took home the Big Ten Conference MVP award. Fullback Pete Johnson scored 26 touchdowns and led the nation with 150 points, and safety Craig

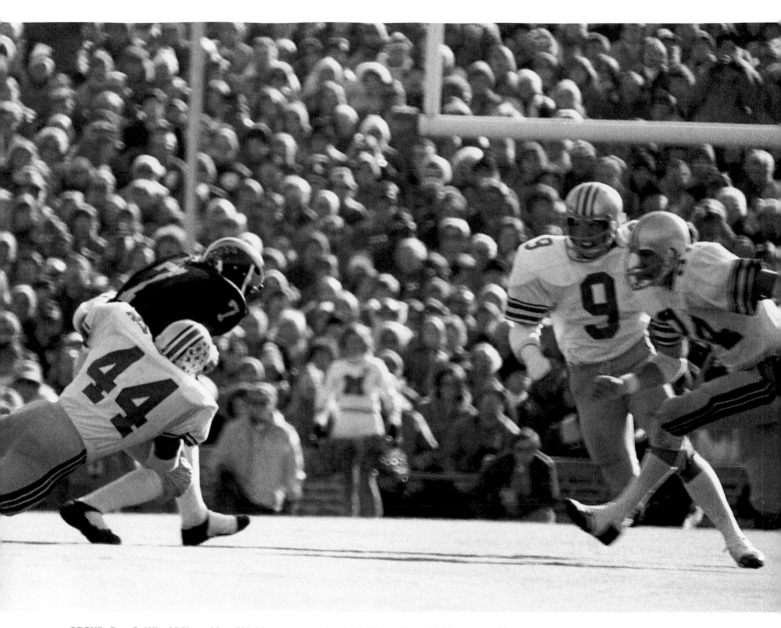

ABOVE: Ray Griffin (44) tackles Michigan quarterback Rick Leach as Ed Thompson (9) and Bob Brudzinski (84) close in to help. (Brockway Sports Photos)

Cassady tied the OSU single-season record of nine interceptions.

While it wasn't the prettiest game for nearly two and a half quarters, the Buckeyes came through when it counted most, snapping Michigan's 41-game home winning streak and, in the process, winning another Big Ten championship. The best part was keeping the Wolverines away from the Rose Bowl yet again.

SCORES BY QUARTERS	1ST	2ND	3RD	4TH	TOTAL
Ohio State	7	0	0	14	21
Michigan	0	7	0	7	14

1st Q-(OSU) Green to Johnson 7-yd TD (7-0 OSU)
2nd Q-(UM) Bell to J. Smith 11-yd TD (7-7)
4th Q-(UM) Leach 1-yd TD (14-7 UM)
4th Q-(OSU) Johnson 1-yd TD (14-14)
4th Q-(OSU) Johnson 3-yd TD (21-14 OSU)

1972

OHIO STATE 14, MICHIGAN 11

Although most fans prefer high-scoring contests, sometimes the best games are low-scoring defensive battles. In saying that, if it is a defensive battle, there better be some big plays to keep the fans on the edges of their seats. The 1972 showdown at Ohio Stadium between the Buckeyes and the Michigan Wolverines proved to be a defensive battle that will not be forgotten any time soon by those who played in it or those who attended the contest.

A cold and rainy November 25 afternoon greeted the 87,040 fans at venerable Ohio Stadium. The Horseshoe, which was celebrating the 50th anniversary since its dedication in 1922, had provided some legendary games in the past. It was about to host another as the Buckeyes welcomed in the "team up north."

Michigan entered the contest at 10-0 overall, 7-0 in league play and ranked third nationally in both the writers' AP poll and the coaches' UPI poll. The Wolverines were riding a 21-game (regular-season) winning streak, 15 straight in the Big Ten. With the conference having abolished its "no repeat" policy at the beginning of the season, a victory over Ohio State would earn the Wolverines a return trip to the Rose Bowl.

Unfortunately for the Buckeyes, two weeks prior, their undefeated season came to a crashing halt as they lost at Michigan State 19-12, ending any hope of both teams playing the season finale unbeaten and untied. Ohio State entered ranked eighth by the UPI and ninth in the AP polls at 8-1 overall, 6-1 in the Big Ten. Many starters from a disappointing 1971 season were back along with several promising sophomores. For the first time in years, the NCAA changed its rule and allowed freshmen to play. One of those freshmen who received significant playing time was running back Archie Griffin, who would later become the only two-time winner of the Heisman Trophy.

The 1972 contest between the Buckeyes and Wolverines marked the fourth meeting between Woody Hayes and Bo Schembechler in their epic 10-year war. Schembechler owned a 2-1 record against his former teacher, including the disputed 10-7 victory the year prior in 1971. Late in that contest, Michigan's Thom Darden intercepted a pass from OSU quarterback Don Lamka at the UM 32-yard line. Darden had leaped over OSU receiver Dick Wakefield to spear the ball. But the Buckeyes and Hayes strongly felt that Darden had interfered with Wakefield. The officials didn't see it that way, and no penalty was called. Feeling his team was being "homered" by the officials, Hayes raced onto the field to protest, where he was flagged for unsportsmanlike conduct and assed a 15-yard penalty. Two plays later, Hayes, still steaming over the "no-call," broke a down marker over his knee and heaved the pieces onto the field. He then proceeded to shred a bright orange first-down indicator on the sidelines. While Woody

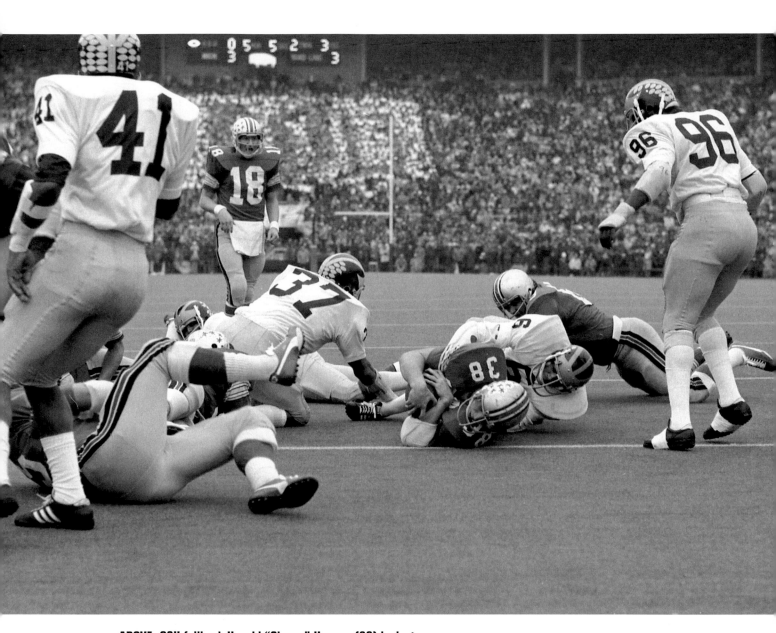

ABOVE: OSU fullback Harold "Champ" Henson (38) looks to score as quarterback Greg Hane (18) watches. Michigan players pictured include Randy Logan (41), Clint Spearman (96) and Tom Kee (37). (Brockway Sports Photos)

refused to speak to the media after the game, Michigan athletic director Don Canham sat down with reporters and said: "Woody's antics and showmanship probably helped draw an additional 30,000 to their games." This only added to the intensity of the rivalry between the two schools.

The fever pitch that had surrounded the 1968 and 1970 OSU-UM games in Columbus wasn't as evident in 1972 since most Ohio State students had gone home to be with their families for Thanksgiving two days before. Nonetheless, it was still Ohio State and Michigan, with a trip to Pasadena on the line. As always, each coach was looking for a psychological edge in an effort to fire up his respective team. In 1968, Ohio State beat Michigan 50-14. Several weeks later, Michigan reassigned head coach Bump Elliott within the athletic department. Then the Wolverines hired Miami of Ohio head coach Bo Schembechler to take over the Michigan program. In 1969, Schembechler decided to hang up the score of the 50-14 loss to OSU on the bathroom door in the locker room. The following year, Woody had his team walk over a carpet with the 24-12 score in the loss to the Wolverines. This season, Coach Hayes had hung up a comment from Michigan quarterback Dennis Franklin, a sophomore quarterback out of Massillon, Ohio, which read: "All Ohio football players don't go to Michigan, only the good ones." Could he have said anything worse to fire up Woody and the boys?

With Big Ten commissioner Wayne Duke in attendance, Michigan went ahead on the third play of the second quarter, 3-0, on Mike Lantry's 35-yard field goal. Ohio State came right back as fullback Harold "Champ" Henson scored his 20th touchdown of the season on a one-yard plunge. Blair Conway

booted the extra point, and the Buckeyes led 7-3 in the second quarter.

As I mentioned earlier, sometimes defensive battles can be great games. Just before halftime, the Ohio State defense put up a goal line stand, the likes of which hadn't been seen since the 1954 win over the Wolverines, when OSU had stopped Michigan on their one-foot line. With Michigan owning a first and goal at the OSU one-yard line, tailback Chuck Heater, out of Tiffin, Ohio, lost a yard, but then regained it on second down. On third down, fullback Bob Thornbladh was stifled as he plunged over right tackle. With the fans screaming at the top of their lungs, Michigan quarterback Dennis Franklin fumbled on the fourth and one, only to recover the ball on the two-yard line, ending the threat. Ohio State went into the locker room leading Michigan 7-3.

Early in the third quarter, Ohio State put together a quick 2:28, 78-yard scoring drive that included two big plays. First, quarterback Greg Hare ran for 35 yards down to the Michigan 30-yard line after keeping the ball on an option. On the next play, Archie Griffin broke through the right tackle, ran right, and faked a Michigan safety out of his jock for a 30-yard touchdown run. Conway's extra point was good, and Ohio State now owned a 14-3 lead.

Sensing that the tide was beginning to turn, Michigan came back with its only touchdown of the day. After driving the length of the field, fullback Ed Shuttlesworth out of Cincinnati powered his way in from one yard out on fourth down for a score. The Wolverines then connected on a two-point conversion as Franklin passed three yards to Clint Haslerig and Michigan cut the Buckeyes' lead down to 14-11.

The Wolverines came knocking again at

Ohio State's goal line early in the fourth quarter after Randy Logan picked off Greg Hare's pass at the Buckeyes' 29-yard line. Several plays later, the OSU defense would be tested again as Michigan moved the ball down to the Buckeyes' five-yard line. On first and goal, Wolverines junior tailback Harry Banks, out of Cleveland, swept right only to be met by OSU defensive back Neil Colzie. Banks, on second and goal from the four, then tried going up the middle, only to be swarmed under by the OSU tackles. Schembechler, determined to score a touchdown, sent Banks through the middle, where Pete Cusick, who had been hospitalized earlier in the week with a virus, stood him up for no gain. Michigan protested to no avail that Banks had scored, but the officials placed the ball just inches short of the goal line. This brought up the game's second fourth and inches at the goal line. The Wolverines went with Franklin on a quarterback sneak up the middle, but OSU linebacker Randy Gradishar was there to grab Franklin, preventing him from scoring the go-ahead touchdown. Gradishar would say in later years: "If Franklin had dove, he would have had the touchdown. But when he ran it, I had a chance to take a step back and hit him."

After OSU stopped Franklin on the fourth and inches, the offense stalled and was forced to punt. Michigan took over in great field position at OSU's 37-yard line. Again, the OSU defense was called upon to make a stop as Franklin's pass on fourth and 11 fell incomplete.

Ohio State's offense finally got on track. With 5:07 left to play in the fourth quarter, Archie Griffin went 15 yards on a pass in the flat from Hare. The Buckeyes then gained a first down followed by an incomplete pass. Michigan was flagged for a personal foul, moving the ball to the Wolverines' 32-yard line with the clock down to two minutes. Three plays later, OSU was faced with a fourth and 11. Hayes elected to kick a field goal, but Blair Conway's 46-yard attempt sailed wide left, giving Michigan one last chance to score.

The second largest crowd in Ohio Stadium history was nearly hysterical. Michigan began one final drive to keep its hopes for an unbeaten season and a trip to the Rose Bowl alive. Ohio State defensive backs Doug Plank and Neil Colzie batted down one pass, Jeff Davis another. Michigan's Bo Rather then caught a pass and went nine yards, setting up Ed Shuttlesworth's dive for a first down. Davis then batted down another Franklin pass before Rather caught two passes, one for 15 yards and another for 14 yards, down to the Buckeyes' 41-yard line. Suddenly, Michigan was nearing field goal range. If they could make a field goal and even the score up at 14-14, the Wolverines, by virtue of a tie, would win the title outright and head to the Rose Bowl.

With under a minute to go, the tension was unbelievable. Michigan had a first and 10 at the Ohio State 41-yard line and everything was on the line. Colzie batted down what might have been a touchdown pass to Wolverines tight end Paul Seal, who was set to grab it at the five with no one in his path. On second down, finding no open receivers, Franklin ran the option for no gain.

With 13 seconds remaining, an unruly mob stormed the field and took down the south goal posts. Fearing repercussions if the game wasn't officially completed, Coach Hayes, along with police officers, tried to restore order on the field. Before the game even began, officials had feared the crowd would run onto the field following an OSU

"We knocked off the third-ranked, undefeated Wolverines in 1972 and nobody ever talks about that. I'm one of the few who can say that he never lost to Michigan, having gone 2-0-1, with the tie coming in 1973. But that win in 1972, with the goal line stands and all, was just great."

—Ohio State offensive lineman John Hicks

victory. As a precaution they had replaced the steel with wooden teardown goal posts. Minutes later, the field cleared of fans, Franklin then ran out of bounds on third down to stop the clock. For the fourth time that day, the Ohio State defense was called upon to stop a Michigan fourth-down attempt. Buckeyes defensive tackle George Hasenohrl then flattened Franklin for no gain. Pandemonium set in as fans took over the field again and the game ended.

Afterwards, the *Columbus Dispatch* described 59-year-old Hayes, with his shirttail hanging out and visibly spent. He told reporters in the locker room he had pulled a calf muscle when he ran onto the field to help save the south goal posts from destruction. Big Ten commissioner Wayne Duke interrupted Hayes's recapitulation of Ohio State's dramatic 14-11 conquest over Michigan to say that spare goal posts had been available and waiting under the grandstand. Hayes chided, "Well, if you had just let me know, you could have saved me a pulled muscle."

The crowd running onto the field towards the end of a game was nothing new in the series. It had happened in years past, but this time, instead of celebrating the crowd

seemed more bent on destruction. Hayes went on to tell the *Columbus Dispatch* and others who had gathered, "Each year it gets a little bit worse. A couple of years ago, I was trying to help out when we had some trouble on campus and one of those people said to me, 'How about the way your football crowd behaves?' And, you know, he had a point. That worried me out there today."

In 2003, former Ohio State offensive lineman John Hicks told WBNS-AM in Columbus, "We knocked off the third-ranked, undefeated Wolverines in 1972 and nobody ever talks about that. I'm one of the few who can say that he never lost to Michigan, having gone 2-0-1, with the tie coming in 1973. But that win in 1972, with the goal line stands and all, was just great."

The experts always say that the stats tell the tale of the game. But in this case, the stats just didn't add up for an Ohio State victory. Michigan led in first downs, 21-10, and total offense, 344 yards to 192. But a critical failure to pound the football into the end zone doomed Michigan. If the Wolverines had gone for a chip-shot field goal attempt on either fourth-down attempt at the OSU goal line and made it, Michigan would have tied the

Buckeyes, thus sending the Wolverines to the Rose Bowl.

Some 30 years later, Schembechler defended his coaching in that game by saying, "On the first goal line stand, I thought we could score from one yard out. We should have scored from there. As far as the second goal line stand, everybody said that Banks had scored on third down when the Ohio crowd was tearing down the posts. I didn't kick the field goal because I felt it was out of our range. Maybe not for some, but it was for us. I was not playing for a tie in this game."

Ohio State's 14-11 victory over Michigan in 1972 was as dramatic as they come. Defensively, OSU put up two goal line stands while batting down passes with the game on the line. Offensively, Henson and Griffin both scored touchdowns. Coach Hayes's pulled calf muscle and the torn goal posts added to the drama. But the most impressive thing of all was the fact that the Ohio State victory ruined Michigan's chances of repeating as undefeated Big Ten champions. The Buckeyes were on their way to the 1973 Rose Bowl.

SCORES BY QUARTER	1ST	2ND	3RD	4TH	TOTAL
Michigan	0	3	8	0	11
Ohio State	0	7	7	0	14

2nd Q-Lantry 35-yd FG (3-0 UM)
2nd Q-Henson 1-yd TD (7-3 OSU)
3rd Q-Griffin 30-yd TD (14-3 OSU)
3rd Q-Shutttlesworth 1-yd TD (UM converts on two-point conversion Franklin to Haslerig 14-11 OSU)

1985

OHIO STATE 22, IOWA 13

Whenever it looks like former Ohio State linebacker Chris Spielman is having a bad day before we go on the air on sports radio "1460 the Fan," in Columbus, Ohio, I'll say to him: "'85 Iowa." Chris's response is generally: "Yeah, it's the best game I ever played in." This response may shock a lot of people, since Spielman was a part of so many big wins during his career, not only at Ohio State, but in the NFL as well. According to Spielman: "Ohio Stadium was a living, breathing entity that day. The crowd was awesome."

Looking back at the November 2, 1985, contest in Ohio Stadium, no one will ever forget the defensive effort the Buckeyes put forth against a powerful Iowa offensive unit or the exploits of backup tailback John Wooldridge.

The week leading up to the showdown between the eighth-ranked Buckeyes and the top-ranked Hawkeyes was dominated by a specific question. Would OSU star tailback Keith Byars be able to play in the biggest game of the year? The senior out of Dayton, Ohio, had bruised his right foot in the win over Minnesota the previous game. It was the same foot that had been broken, forcing him to miss the first four games of the season. In 1984, Byars, the Big Ten's defending rushing and scoring champion, had a remarkable game against the Hawkeyes. He rushed for two

touchdowns, caught a touchdown pass while tossing another in Ohio State's 45-26 victory over Iowa. When pressed during the week by *Columbus Dispatch* reporter Tim May, OSU head coach Earle Bruce's response was: "He didn't practice again today. You could say he is doubtful to out. I would say he is out."

If Byars couldn't play on Saturday, the starting tailback job would fall to freshman Vince Workman out of Dublin, Ohio, splitting time with John Wooldridge. Big fullback George Cooper would pave the way with his monster blocks for whoever ended up behind him in the backfield. Unknown to many, Wooldridge had been suffering from severely bruised ribs. Realizing that Byars might not play and the Buckeyes' offense would be limited to only a freshman tailback in the backfield, Wooldridge knew he had to overcome the pain, "I was a senior, we were hosting top-ranked Iowa, and Byars was down. I had to play. I just had to. I couldn't lay all that on a freshman."

With the focus on whether or not Byars would play against Iowa, an equally important story was out there as well. Would Ohio State's defense be able to stop, or at least slow down, Iowa's potent passing attack? The Hawkeyes' senior quarterback, Chuck Long, led the nation in passing efficiency, having thrown for 1,984 yards, 21 touchdowns and eight inter-

OPPOSITE: Tailback John Wooldridge in the midst of his 57-yard touchdown run in the second quarter. (Brockway Sports Photos)

ceptions. Iowa also had all-purpose running back Ronnie Harmon, who was fifth nationally with a 170.4-yard average. Ohio State's defense ranked ninth in pass defense in the Big Ten and seventh in total defense, a huge concern for the coaching staff, fans and the media.

Fortunately for Ohio State, they led the Big Ten conference games in scoring, averaging 35 points per game with junior quarterback Jim Karsatos at the helm. With the talented Byars keeping defenses honest with a ferocious rushing attack, Karsatos quietly put together a nice season throwing the ball. The junior out of southern California, ranked fifth nationally in passing efficiency with 1,247 yards, with 14 touchdowns to only four interceptions. For the first time since the 1977 game against Oklahoma, Ohio State was an underdog in Ohio Stadium. The 7-0 top-ranked Hawkeyes were a one and a half-point favorite over eighth-ranked Ohio State (6-1). The Buckeyes were riding a 19-game home winning streak while the Hawkeyes were trying to win at the "Horseshoe" for the first time since 1959.

On November 2, 1985, a record sellout crowd of 90,467 was on hand at cold and rainy Ohio Stadium to watch number-one Iowa battle the eighth-ranked Buckeyes. It would turn out to be one of the all-time greatest games in OSU football history. While the crowd was hyped up in the stands, the Buckeyes had become fired up before they ever walked onto the field. Before the game, it was learned that running back Keith Byars would not be able to play due to his severely bruised right foot. That didn't keep him from giving one of the most memorable pregame speeches in OSU history. According to Wooldridge: "Byars fired us up in our pregame meal and got us to understand the importance of the game in both the Big Ten standings and national standings, for that matter. In order to show us he was into the game from a mental standpoint, he got so wound up and so tense that he swiped at the table—all of our plates, bowls and glasses went flying across the room and shattered all over the place—before kicking a chair. We realized that Byars may not be in the game physically, but emotionally and mentally he was right there, and we needed to be right there with him."

Ohio State got on the scoreboard first as Rich Spangler booted a 28-yard field goal to make it 3-0 Ohio State. Following a good OSU defensive stand that pinned Iowa near its own goal line, Ohio State roverback Sonny Gordon blocked an Iowa punt out of the end zone for a safety. The Buckeyes now had a 5-0 lead.

Early in the second quarter, OSU defensive back William White picked off a Chuck Long pass and returned it to the Buckeyes' 38-yard line. Then, on his first carry of the day, Wooldridge ripped off a 57-yard touchdown run. Spangler's extra point was good and the Buckeyes had a shocking 12-0 lead over the top-ranked Hawkeyes with 9:06 left before halftime.

Defensively, Ohio State befuddled Long, the nation's top passer. The senior was never able to get on track, having thrown first-half interceptions to Spielman, White and Greg Rogan. Rogan's theft set up Spangler's 26-yard field goal, giving Ohio State a 15-0 lead.

Iowa was finally able to put some points on the scoreboard late in the second quarter as the Hawkeyes drove 88 yards on 14 plays for a touchdown. Running back Ronnie Harmon scored from three yards out on an option pitch to the left as Iowa closed the gap to 15-7 with just 28 seconds remaining before halftime.

The third quarter was scoreless, but as the game progressed, Ohio State's defense became

ABOVE: OSU linebacker Chris Spielman (36) tackles Ronnie Harmon (31) as Eric Krumerow (14) rushes in to help. (Ohio State University Photo Archive)

stronger and stronger. Iowa safety Jay Norvell set up a potential go-ahead score for the Hawkeyes by picking off a Karsatos pass and returning it seven yards down to OSU's 19-yard line. Harmon then carried the ball twice, down to the Ohio State 11-yard line. On third down, OSU linebacker Pepper Johnson fired through and nailed Harmon at the ten-yard line. Instead of attempting a 27-yard field goal, Iowa head coach Hayden Fry opted to go for the first down. On fourth and one, Spielman, playing the game of his life, nailed Harmon for no gain as the Buckeyes held.

Ohio State and Iowa then traded touchdowns in the fourth quarter. Derek Isaman knocked a ball loose from receiver Scott Halverson, which Fred Ridder recovered at

the Iowa 31. This set up Workman's touchdown from four yards out to give the Buckeyes a 22-7 lead. Iowa answered with an 80-yard drive capped off with a touchdown by David Hudson. In the hopes of cutting OSU's lead down to just seven points, Iowa went for two points, but failed when Kevin Harmon, who was in for his injured brother Ronnie, was stopped by Gordon.

With less than four minutes left, Iowa was on the move again deep in Ohio State territory at the 25-yard line. Long's pass over the middle at the five-yard line fell incomplete as the ball touched the fingertips of Quinn Early before he was blasted by OSU defensive back Terry White. Early popped back up after the play, while White lay on the ground, the wind knocked out of him. Iowa's Rob Houghtlin then missed a 42-yard field goal, as the score remained 22-13, Ohio State.

On Iowa's final possession, Spielman picked off his second pass of the day to seal the victory. Ohio State then ran out the clock as the Buckeyes completed a stunning victory over the top-ranked Hawkeyes, 22-13. On the rain-soaked Astroturf, the Buckeyes jumped for joy while others rolled around on the field as the wild celebration took place. For the second time in 17 years, the Buckeyes had upset a top-ranked team in Ohio Stadium. The other was Purdue on October 12, 1968. Ironically enough, 50 years before to the day, November 2, 1935, Ohio State had lost a late lead before being stunned by Notre Dame 18-13, in what many experts would call the greatest game in the first 50 years of college football.

After the game, Bruce told the *Columbus Dispatch:* "We won it in November last year. It happened last year and it can happen again this year." If the Buckeyes could defeat Northwestern, Wisconsin and Michigan in their final three games, the Buckeyes would be back in the Rose Bowl for a second consecutive year. According to Cooper: "No more nine-and-threes," he said, referring to Ohio State's record each of the last five seasons. Unfortunately, after beating Northwestern, the Buckeyes would lose their final two games to Wisconsin and Michigan. Ohio State wound up in the Citrus Bowl, where they beat Brigham Young University by a final of 10-7—to finish up at 9-3.

The true heroes of the day were the members of the Ohio State defense. The Buckeyes stifled the country's best passer in Long, intercepting him four times, two times by Spielman. Long, who had been averaging 324 yards per game passing, was held to only 169 yards passing along with the four picks.

Seventeen of the Buckeyes' 22 points resulted from Iowa turnovers. Spielman and Johnson each recorded 19 tackles on the afternoon.

Besides recording 19 tackles and intercepting two passes, the legend of Spielman was beginning to take off. At one point in the game, the pads inside his helmet popped off, causing his helmet to fly off. Following the play, Spielman's request of the referee to stop the action for an equipment timeout was denied. According to Spielman: "The ref wouldn't give me an equipment timeout, so on the next play, with Long rolling out, my helmet was bobbing up and down on my head. So I just said, 'The heck with it' and I threw it off and went after him." So much for getting flagged for not having your equipment secured while on the field.

Offensively, Wooldridge ripped off a 57-yard touchdown run, thanks to a huge block by Cooper. Cooper became the first Ohio State fullback to rush for over 100 yards in a game (104) since Ricardo Volley had 132 yards against Michigan in 1979. Karsatos completed 10-17 passes for 157 yards with two interceptions, while Workman added a touchdown in place of the injured Byars.

This dramatic victory over top-ranked Iowa would prove to be the highlight of the 1985 season.

SCORES BY QUARTERS	1ST	2ND	3RD	4TH	TOTAL
Iowa	0	7	0	6	13
Ohio State	5	10	0	7	22

1st Q-(OSU) Spangler 28-yd FG (3-0 OSU)
1st Q-(OSU) Kostrubala punt blocked out of endzone (Gordon for OSU-5-0 OSU)
2nd Q-(OSU) Wooldridge 57-yd TD (12-0 OSU)
2nd Q-(OSU) Spangler 26-yd FG (15-0 OSU)
2nd Q-(IA) R. Harmon 3-yd TD (15-7 OSU)
4th Q-(OSU) Workman 4-yd TD (22-7 OSU)
4th Q-(IA) Hudson 2-yd TD (Two-point conversion failed—22-13 OSU)

**ABOVE: OSU safety Sonny Gordon (7) blocks Iowa's Greg Kostrubali's (27) punt
for a safety. (Ohio State University Photo Archive)**

1961

OHIO STATE 50, MICHIGAN 20

Imagine if you will that your team is on the verge of going to its third Rose Bowl in the past eight seasons with a win at Michigan. Sound pretty good? Usually, that would be a great season, unless your own faculty council voted not to allow you to participate. That dose of reality hung over the heads of everyone connected with the Ohio State football program in the weeks leading up to the annual showdown with the Wolverines in 1961.

In 1946, an agreement was signed between the Big Ten Conference and the Pacific Eight Conference that allowed the conference champions to meet in the Rose Bowl each January 1. But in 1959, the Big Ten split their votes, five for and five against, on renewing the agreement. This meant that following the 1960 Rose Bowl, the contract between the two conferences would come to an end.

The following season, Minnesota won the Big Ten title. Although the contract between the two conferences had run out, the Rose Bowl invited the Gophers to play Washington in the New Year's Day bowl.

In the fall of 1961, everyone fully expected Ohio State to be an outstanding team. 26 lettermen returned to a squad coming off a 7-2 record in 1960. The question was, would OSU's faculty allow the Buckeyes to play in the Rose Bowl if they should capture the Big Ten title?

The Buckeyes started out with a season-opening 7-7 tie with TCU. The following week, OSU won out on the west coast by beating UCLA, 13-3. Ohio State then opened up Big Ten play by shutting out Illinois and Northwestern in consecutive weeks before rolling up conference victories over Wisconsin, Iowa and Indiana. OSU beat Oregon, 22-12 in a nonconference game before the yearly showdown with Michigan.

On the Friday following Thanksgiving, Ohio State traveled north to enemy territory to face Michigan in Ann Arbor. Under third-year head coach Bump Elliot, the Wolverines entered the contest at 6-2 overall, 3-2 in the Big Ten. OSU was 7-0-1 overall, 5-0 in the conference. OSU was favored by one point in the contest by the experts. Meanwhile, Minnesota was also going for an undefeated Big Ten campaign as they battled Wisconsin at Camp Randall Stadium in Madison. If OSU could beat Michigan coupled with a Wisconsin upset at home over the Gophers, the Buckeyes would win an outright Big Ten championship.

On November 25, 1961, over 80,000 fans showed up at the "Big House" to watch the annual grudge match. Ohio State scored the first points with 3:26 left to go in the first quarter as fullback Bob Ferguson broke over the middle for a 19-yard touchdown run. Dick Van Raaphorst kicked the extra point to give OSU a 7-0 lead.

ABOVE: OSU fullback Bob Ferguson (46) falls inches shy of scoring one of his four touchdowns on the afternoon. (Brockway Sports Photos)

Following a Michigan fumble early in the second quarter, the Buckeyes' offense went back on the attack. Seven plays later, Ferguson rumbled in for his second score of the day. Following the extra point, Ohio State led, 14-0.

On the ensuing kickoff, Dayton, Ohio, native Davey Ramey brought the fans to their feet and Michigan back into the game. Ramey received the kickoff at Michigan's 10-yard line and proceeded down the east sideline, dodging Buckeye players before breaking into the clear at his own 40-yard line. From that point on it was a foot race, with the speedy Ramey going all 90 yards for the Wolverines' first score of the day. Ramey's spectacular run remains to this day the only kickoff to be returned for a touchdown in series history. The Wolverines decided to go for two, but the pass fell incomplete and the scored stayed at 14-6.

With 10:49 left in the second quarter, the Buckeyes downed the ensuing kickoff in the end zone to start their next drive on the 20-yard line. Four plays later at their own 31-yard line, one of the most electrifying plays in the history of the vaunted series took place. Ohio State sophomore halfback Paul Warfield, out of Warren, Ohio, swept right on a new counter play, faking the Michigan safety off his feet and going 69 yards for a touchdown.

To this day, Warfield's 69-yard scamper remains the second longest run from scrimmage in an Ohio State-Michigan game. Following the extra point, OSU led, 21-6, with 5:56 left in the second quarter, a lead that stood until halftime.

Following halftime, Michigan put together a monster drive to start off the third quarter. With 8:26 left in the third quarter, Michigan punched it in on a fourth and one at OSU's one-yard line, completing a 78-yard march that saw them use up nearly seven min-

utes. The two-point conversion failed again, but Michigan had chopped the Buckeyes' lead down to 21-12.

Despite leading by nine points, Ohio State desperately needed a drive of its own for two reasons. First, the Buckeyes needed to give their defense a break. Second, they needed stop the shift in momentum that the Wolverines were starting to experience while playing in front of their own crowd. OSU took over at its 20-yard line and proceeded to put together a drive that ended any hopes of a Michigan victory that day.

On fourth and three at Michigan's 19-yard line, Ferguson crashed through the middle for five yards and a first down at Michigan's 14-yard line. On the next play, Ferguson went over left tackle for 12 more yards down to UM's two. Quarterback Joe Sparma again handed the ball off to Ferguson, who gained one more yard, down to the one-yard line, as time expired in the third quarter. At the end of three quarters, OSU led Michigan, 21-12.

One of the greatest quarters in Ohio State history was about to take place. Two plays into the fourth quarter, Bob Ferguson slanted off right tackle for a touchdown. The extra point was good and OSU led, 28-12. Ferguson had carried the ball nine times for 30 yards and a touchdown. The big play in the drive was a 37-yard run by Warfield.

Michigan, now desperate for a score to stay in the game, tossed an interception that was picked off by Ron Houck at Ohio State's 14-yard line, returning it down to the Wolverines' 21. Three plays later, Sparma found right halfback Bob Klein for six more points, and following the extra point, OSU led, 35-12.

The OSU defense held Michigan to a three-and-out series before taking over again at the 50. In typical Hayes fashion, OSU began to pound the ball with its big fullback. Ferguson proceeded to run the ball for 10 and then 25 yards down to Michigan's 15. Three plays later, Ferguson rumbled into the end zone from one yard out for his fourth score of the day. Dick Van Raaphorst booted his sixth extra point of the afternoon as the Buckeyes led, 42-12.

The Wolverines were able to score a touchdown and a two-point conversion with 34 seconds remaining in the contest to make it 42-20 Ohio State. That's the way most figured the game would end. OSU would take the kickoff, run one play and end the contest with a victory. Much to everyone's amazement, Sparma tossed the ball 70 yards to a streaking Warfield, who took the ball down to Michigan's 10-yard line with just 14 seconds remaining. Michigan's players and fans were stunned. Why would Ohio State do this with the game out of hand and under a minute to go in the contest? Sparma then tossed two more passes that fell incomplete. With just five seconds remaining, Sparma then found end Sam Tidmore, who twisted and flailed his way in for the final touchdown of the afternoon. The Buckeyes then decided to go for two as Sparma connected with Tidmore again to make it 50-20.

Later, Ohio State head coach Woody Hayes was asked about running up the score on their hated rivals. He denied that the final touchdown and two-point conversion had anything to do with "getting even" for the 58-6 shellacking Michigan handed Ohio State in 1946. The *Columbus Dispatch* quoted Hayes afterwards as saying: "The Bucks don't get steamed up on junk like that; 58-6, so what. One writer accused me of running up the score on Bump [Elliot]. I might do that to Fritz Crisler, but not Bump. Bump Elliot is truly one of the great sportsmen in football."

As far as the two-point conversion, Hayes laughed: "The boys talked me into it. They said, 'Let's get 50.'"

With five seconds left in the game, OSU kicked off to Michigan, which returned the ball to its 35-yard line as time expired. Just as in 1955 when the Buckeyes had beaten the Wolverines in Ann Arbor, thousands of fans stormed the field in assault of the goal posts. Hayes was carried off the field on the shoulders of his players as they rushed for the locker room. While the Buckeyes ran off, numerous fights were breaking out on the field between the schools fans.

Meanwhile, in Minneapolis, Jim Bakken's 31-yard field goal with 3:57 remaining lifted Wisconsin past the Golden Gophers, 23-21. That, coupled with Ohio State winning at Michigan, gave the Buckeyes an outright Big Ten championship at 7-0. Minnesota finished conference play at 6-1. For Hayes, it was his fourth unbeaten Big Ten championship campaign in 11 seasons at Ohio State.

The Ohio State offense rolled up one of the biggest days ever against a Michigan defense. OSU led in first downs, 22-16, and in total offensive yards, 512-271. The 50 points were the most ever scored by an OSU team against Michigan (later to be equaled in 1968). Ferguson carried the ball 30 times for 152 yards and four touchdowns. Warfield had his best day as a Buckeye, breaking through for just over 200 yards in total offense, which included a 69-yard run for a score along with a 70-yard reception. Klein and Tidmore also scored on the day, while Van Raaphorst booted six extra points. Tidmore also scored on a two-point conversion.

Following the win in the locker room, Hayes was asked whether or not the Buckeyes would be allowed to play in the Rose Bowl if invited? Hayes responded by telling the *Dispatch*, "I'm not saying anything publicly about that right now."

"I took **a long walk** to cool off, afraid of what [I] might say."

—Coach Woody Hayes

On Monday, November 27, Ohio State was voted past Alabama to the number one ranking in the polls. The next day, the dreaded vote by OSU's faculty council took place. Feeling that football was becoming too powerful, the council, in a secret ballot, voted 28 to 25, rejecting an informal invitation for the Big Ten champion Buckeyes to play in the January 1, 1962, Rose Bowl against Pac-8 champion UCLA.

Hayes was in Cleveland when he found out about the "no-vote." He was nearly an hour and a half late for his speaking engagement that night to the OSU alumni gathered at the Hollendon Hotel, telling the *Columbus Dispatch:* "I took a long walk to cool off, afraid of what [I] might say." Hayes told the assembled crowd, "I don't agree with those 28 no-voters, but I respect their integrity, if not their intelligence."

While Coach Hayes took the high road in Cleveland, students on the Ohio State campus started to demonstrate, first by hanging and burning in effigy those who had apparently blocked OSU's Rose Bowl appearance. Then, some 5,000 students marched to the state capitol to protest. City buses, several businesses, and police cars were damaged along the way as the students showed their displeasure walking down High Street.

The protests continued into Wednesday night. The *Dispatch* reported that OSU football captain Mike Ingram helped authorities break up a demonstration at 15th and High Street by speaking over a police cruiser loudspeaker. Ingram told the crowd: "The team did all of the work. If we can accept the decision, you certainly can! Now go home." With those words, the crowd finally left.

Ohio State would wait seven years before winning another Big Ten title. Opposing coaches used the OSU faculty council's "no-vote" against Hayes in recruiting. The "no-vote" undoubtedly hurt the Buckeyes in recruiting for the next several years and nearly cost Hayes his job in 1967.

SCORES BY QUARTER	1ST	2ND	3RD	4TH	TOTAL
Ohio State	7	14	0	29	50
Michigan	0	6	6	8	20

1st Q-(OSU) Ferguson 19-yd TD (7-0 OSU)
2nd Q-(OSU) Ferguson 1-yd TD (14-0 OSU)
2nd Q-(UM) Raimey 90-yd K.O. Return for a TD (two-point conversion failed, 14-6 OSU)
2nd Q-(OSU) Warfield 69-yd TD (21-6 OSU)
3rd Q-(UM) McLenna 1-yd TD (two-point conversion failed, 21-12 OSU)
4th Q-(OSU) Ferguson 1-yd TD (28-12 OSU)
4th Q-(OSU) Sparma to Klein 80-yd TD (35-12 OSU)
4th Q-(OSU) Ferguson 1-yd TD (42-12 OSU)
4th Q-(UM) Ward 1-yd TD (Two point conversion good, 42-20 OSU)
4th Q-(OSU) Sparma to Tidmore 10-yd (Two point conversion good, 50-20 OSU)

1979

OHIO STATE 18, MICHIGAN 15

When Ohio State played at Michigan on November 17, 1979, the classic rivalry was the same, but an icon was missing. It was "The Game" against the "Team from up North," but for the first time since 1951, Woody Hayes wasn't on the sidelines for the Buckeyes. Ever since that fateful December 29 night in 1978, when Coach Hayes was fired after punching Clemson linebacker Charlie Bauman in the Gator Bowl, Ohio State football would be never be quite the same.

Immediately after the Gator Bowl game, Ohio State University president Harold Enarson and athletic director Hugh Hindman fired Hayes, thus ending his 28-year run as head coach of the Ohio State Buckeyes. The university began a nationwide search for a new coach. On January 12, 1979, to everyone's surprise, the university hired former player and assistant coach Earle Bruce. The 47-year-old Bruce, who served as an assistant under Hayes from 1966-71, had been the head coach at Iowa State since 1973. Twice in six seasons, Bruce had been named the Big 8 Coach of the Year, taking lowly Iowa State to 8-3 records in two of the last three seasons.

In his first season at Ohio State, Bruce had his work cut out in rebuilding the Buckeyes, who had gone 7-4-1 in 1978 and had lost the previous three seasons to Michigan. With only 11 returning starters, including sophomore quarterback Art Schlichter, no one could have predicted the success ahead of the 1979 Buckeyes. On September 8, Ohio State start-ed the season by clobbering Syracuse, 31-8. The following week, the Buckeyes trailed at Minnesota, 14-0, before winning their conference opener, 21-17. Ohio State then beat Washington State, 45-29, and UCLA, 17-13. OSU returned home and had another close call on October 6, beating Northwestern in a lackluster game, 16-7. The Buckeyes then began to click both offensively and defensively, winning their next five games by an average score of 45-4. Everything was lining up perfectly for the finale at Michigan.

Ohio State entered its final game of the season at Michigan at 10-0, ranked second in the weekly AP poll while Michigan was ranked 13th, at 8-2. While the game was as big as ever, the Buckeyes didn't necessarily have to win to play in the Rose Bowl. First, a victory would give Ohio State a perfect 11-0 record and an outright Big Ten title. A loss to Michigan coupled with a Purdue win at Indiana, and the Buckeyes, Wolverines and Boilermakers would be locked for a three-way tie for first in the conference, sending OSU to the Rose Bowl by virtue of a better overall record.

Hayes had gone 16-11-1 against the Wolverines, but had lost the last three matchups without scoring a touchdown. The famous 10-year war against his protégé Bo Schembechler had ended with Bo having the upper hand at 5-4-1. A new war between Schembechler and Bruce was about to begin, with Michigan hoping to ruin the Buckeyes'

ABOVE: First-year OSU football coach Earle Bruce is set to lead his team onto the field in Ann Arbor. (Brockway Sports Photos)

perfect record while extending its winning streak over OSU to four straight.

Before heading to Ann Arbor, Coach Bruce extended a gracious offer to his former boss, Woody Hayes, to speak to the players at Senior Tackle. Hayes accepted and spoke to the team with nearly 1,000 fans in attendance. Paul Hornung of the *Columbus Dispatch* quoted Hayes as saying:

"It's the greatest single game in history. High school, college and pro athletics. It's played by teams representing two great educational institutions; they're almost always vying for that championship, and they're always great football teams. The Super Bowl is a great game, but who's going to be in it next year? Nobody knows. You can't build up a head of steam until the season's all over. But this Michigan game, you start building up a head of steam for next year's game tomorrow, about four o'clock. The memory of that game will stay with you forever. I have no doubt this team, with the great, great coaching it's had this year and the way these players have responded to coach Bruce and his coaches, I have no doubt that this team will come back from Ann Arbor the lone champion of…" His sentence was then drowned out by applause and chants of approval from the crowd.

Former OSU running back Calvin Murray remembered that day, saying: "Coach Hayes lined up on the track beyond the blocking sled and shook hands with each of the 21 seniors following their final 'tackle.' He said something to each one as they finished, with some of the players wrapping their arms around his shoulders. I thought that was really nice of him to do that." Following "Senior Tackle," Bruce convinced Hayes to dine with the team at the Ohio State University Golf Course for its traditional dinner, where the players warmly received him.

Almost every year, whether the game is held at Ohio Stadium, or in this case, Michigan Stadium, a new attendance record is set. In 1979, the largest crowd in college football history, 106,255 fans, packed into "The Big House" to watch Ohio State take on the Michigan Wolverines. Ohio State was looking to wrap up an outright Big Ten title while improving to 11-0. Michigan was hoping to win its fourth consecutive game against Ohio State and, in the process, ruin the Buckeyes' shot at a perfect season and perhaps a national title.

Ohio State put the first points of the day on the scoreboard early in the second quarter when kicker Vlade Janakievski booted a 23-yard field goal. Michigan answered with a 59-yard touchdown strike from quarterback John Wangler to receiver Anthony Carter to make it 7-3 Wolverines. Then, Bruce did something Hayes never did, and that's call for seven consecutive passes, completing four as OSU drove the ball back down the field. Schlichter's key passes were a 25-yarder to Doug Donley and a 22-yarder to Gary Williams. The Buckeyes then settled for a 25-yard field goal by Janakievski with only eight seconds remaining before halftime to pull within a point at 7-6. Although the score didn't indicate it, OSU's offense had moved the ball five times inside the Wolverines' 40-yard line, but accounted for only six points.

Early in the second half, following an interception of an Schlichter pass, Michigan blew a chance to put up another seven points as Ohio State stuffed the Wolverines on fourth and inches at the OSU two-yard line. Before the play could develop, OSU's Marcus Marek and Al Washington nailed Michigan quarterback Rick Hewlett at the Ohio State four-yard line.

"We're going to the Rose Bowl, the right way."

—Head coach Earle Bruce

Early in the fourth quarter, the Buckeyes did something that they hadn't been able to do against Michigan since 1975—score a touchdown. Quarterback Art Schlichter found receiver Chuck Hunter on an 18-yard touchdown pass that put the Buckeyes in front, 12-7, ending 15 consecutive quarters without a touchdown against the Wolverines. It was a beautiful touchdown catch by Hunter as Michigan's Mike Jolly tipped the pass before Hunter was able to make a leaping catch in the corner of the end zone for the score. Ahead by only five points, OSU decided to go for the two-point conversion, which failed.

In typical Michigan fashion, the Wolverines responded with an 80-yard touchdown drive to take back the lead. First, Wangler found Carter on a 66-yard pass before Roosevelt Smith muscled his way into the end zone from a yard out. Knowing that an Ohio State field goal would give the Buckeyes the lead, and possible victory, Michigan opted to go for a two-point conversion, which they made. The Wolverines took a 15-12 lead after three quarters.

Every team has an Achilles heel, and the job of the opposition is to expose and exploit the soft spot to their advantage. In some cases, the opposing team's Achilles' heel is obvious; sometimes, only a great coaching staff can find it in mounds of game films. In the case of Michigan, its punting game was an obvious weak point. Late in the fourth quarter, OSU forced Michigan to punt deep in its own ter-ritory. One of the biggest plays in the history of Ohio State football was about to take place. With OSU rushing 10 men, linebacker Jim Laughlin broke through Michigan's line untouched and blocked Brian Virgil's punt. Safety Todd Bell scooped the ball up and raced 18 yards for the touchdown, giving Ohio State an 18-15 lead. Inexplicably, Janakievski missed the all-important point after, hooking it to the right, and the Buckeyes' lead remained at 18-15. Ohio State's defense was able to hold Michigan the rest of the way as the Buckeyes defeated the Wolverines 18-15 for their first victory over "The team up north" since 1975. The win sent OSU to their first Rose Bowl appearance in four years.

Afterwards, in a wild Ohio State locker room, linebacker Jim Laughlin told reporters, including the *Columbus Dispatch:* "I wasn't touched. Nobody touched me. The ball hit me on both forearms as it came off his [Michigan punter Bryan Virgil] foot." Safety Todd Bell added: "Vince Skillings tried to pick it up, but he fumbled it. I picked it up and ran it in."

Ohio State head coach Earle Bruce, who had been carried off the field in celebration, told reporters: "We're going to the Rose Bowl, the right way." Ohio State's win coupled with Purdue's 37-21 victory at Indiana locked up an outright Big Ten championship for the first year OSU coach in dramatic style. Bruce would later tell the *Columbus Dispatch:* "In great, great football games, the kicking game has a great deal to do with it. The

blocked punt played a big part in our success today. We rushed 10 men on the play. Earlier, we showed a 10-man rush, but dropped out of it and they passed [from punt formation]. We figured that they wouldn't pass again, so we went after them."

At the 2004 Columbus Touchdown Club's 49th annual awards banquet, Murray remembered the game, saying: "It was one of the greatest games I was able to be a part of. I was actually injured at that time with a hip pointer, but I did have a big run early on and caught a couple of passes. The electricity of the game, beating Michigan and finally getting my gold pants, it was outstanding."

The victory over Michigan signified a new beginning at Ohio State. Under Bruce, the Buckeyes were able to put behind a horrible ending to the 1978 season while also ending three consecutive years of losing to the Wolverines. Following 28 seasons under the legendary Hayes, Bruce was able to quickly establish himself as the right man for the job while earning Coach of the Year honors.

SCORES BY QUARTERS	1ST	2ND	3RD	4TH	TOTAL
Ohio State	0	6	6	6	18
Michigan	0	7	8	0	15

2nd Q-(OSU) Janakievski 21-yd FG (3-0 OSU)
2nd Q-(UM) Wangler 59-yd TD pass to Carter (7-3 UM)
2nd Q-(OSU) Janakievski 25-yd FG (7-6 OSU)
3rd Q-(OSU) Schlichter 18-yd TD pass to Hunter (OSU two-point conversion failed, Schlichter's pass failed, 12-7 OSU)
3rd Q-(UM) Smith 1-yd TD (UM two-point conversion good, Smith run, 15-12 UM)
4th Q-(OSU) Bell 18-yd return of a blocked punt for a TD (Janakievski kick failed 18-15 OSU)

1954

Ohio State 31, Wisconsin 14

Some fans disregard games that happened a half century ago because they either hadn't been born yet or are too young to remember. This shouldn't be the case. I must give kudos to the voters for putting Ohio State's 1954 showdown against Wisconsin in our top 25.

Entering the 1954 season, many fans and media felt it was a "make or break" season for head coach Woody Hayes. Previous head coach Wes Fesler had resigned following the 1950 loss to Michigan in the famous "Snow Bowl." Many fans had hoped that either former OSU head coach Paul Brown or Missouri coach Don Faurot would be hired to take over for Fesler. Faurot reportedly accepted the job, only to change his mind and stay at Missouri. The search committee turned to Hayes, who had been the head coach at Miami of Ohio since 1949.

Coach Hayes's first three seasons were average at best. In 1951, the Buckeyes went 4-3-2 with a loss to Michigan. The following season in 1952, OSU improved to 6-3 overall with a victory over Michigan, good for third place in the Big Ten Conference. In 1953, OSU finished in fourth place in the conference, 6-3 overall with a 20-0 loss at Michigan. Most felt that 1954 would be Coach Hayes's final season if things didn't improve.

Not much was expected from the Buckeyes in 1954. OSU was picked to finish in fifth place in the Big Ten Conference. Knowing that his job was on the line, Hayes produced one of the greatest single-season coaching performances in school history.

Ohio State started off its season with wins over Indiana, California, Illinois and Iowa. In the home victory over Iowa, Paul Hornung, the late sports editor for the *Columbus Dispatch,* wrote: "Ohio State's fighting football machine, super-charged with high octane of the finest spirit in years, put the brakes on two would-be Iowa touchdown drives in the fourth period to preserve a 20-14 victory Saturday, before 82,131 breathless Ohio Stadium fans. So overjoyed were the Buckeyes as the final second ticked off the clock, they tossed their helmets in the air; reserves poured from the bench to mob the active players and the squad bore Hayes triumphantly off the gridiron on its shoulders."

After the game Hayes praised sophomore fullback/linebacker Hubert Bobo from Chancey-Dover: "His leadership is just unbelievable," Hayes said. "He's the greatest competitor I've ever coached and his spirit is infectious."

If there ever was a player built to satisfy Hayes, Bobo was the man. Hayes recalled Bobo's attitude during the summer of 1954 as an example during a football class on the field during the summer quarter. According to the *Dispatch:* "I've never seen a boy work any harder or enjoy it more. One day it was 104 degrees and rivers of sweat were running off of him. Everybody in the class was practically dead, but he acted like he loved it. I called for

ABOVE: OSU football coach Woody Hayes is carried off the field following the victory over Wisconsin. Also pictured are Dave Leggett (22) and Jack Archer (16). (Ohio State University Photo Archive)

everyone to take a blow. 'Aw, Coach, let's not stop now,' Bobo complained. 'Let's run a couple of more plays.' How can you beat a guy like that?"

For the first time in four seasons under Coach Hayes, Ohio State had started off a season a perfect 4-0. The stage was now set for a major showdown on October 23 against the second-ranked Wisconsin Badgers. Both teams entered the game at 4-0. The Badgers had the league's best defense while the Buckeyes had the Big Ten's top offense.

Ohio State, having already beaten conference foes Indiana, Illinois and Iowa, stood at 3-0 in Big Ten play, 4-0 overall. Wisconsin entered at 2-0 in the conference, 4-0 overall. The Badgers were ranked second in the nation while OSU was ranked fourth. A Homecoming Day crowd of 82,626 fans was ready to watch one of the biggest games in years at Ohio Stadium. A record 400 press passes were issued to sports writers and sportscasters from all over the country to cover one of the top games in the nation.

Fullback Alan Ameche and veteran quarterback Jim Miller, along with longtime coach Ivy Williamson, led the Badgers. Williamson had taken the Wisconsin program to a 34-12-4 record during his six seasons. The only team the Badgers had not defeated during that time was Ohio State. Williamson stood at 0-4-1 against the Buckeyes and reportedly considered the upcoming game as a "personal challenge," because he hadn't beaten OSU.

In a punishing first half of football, Ohio State grabbed an early 3-0 lead before Wisconsin scored a touchdown for a 7-3 advantage at intermission. During the first half, Coach Hayes wore a coat and baseball cap. In the second half, the hat and coat were gone. Meanwhile on the Wisconsin sideline, Coach Williamson, dressed in a brown sports coat and darker brown pants, gave no signs of emotion, standing most of the time, smoking cigarettes, with his hands on his hips.

Late in the third quarter with Wisconsin on the Buckeyes' 20, Howard "Hopalong" Cassady made one of the greatest single plays in OSU history. With Wisconsin facing a second and four at OSU's 20, Cassady intercepted Miller's pass at the Ohio State 12-yard line. Behind several key blocks, Cassady brought the capacity crowd to its feet by zigging and zagging his way back 88 yards for a touchdown.

The gutsy halfback out of Columbus Central High School played with a gash over his nose, nearly broken in the win over Iowa the week prior. His right hand was encased in a sponge bandage to cover a four-stitch wound. It didn't matter, though. Like so many other legends who had played at Ohio State, Cassady put aside his personal injuries for the greater good of the team. He would later tell the *Columbus Dispatch:* "I just grabbed the ball and took off running."

Some 50 years later, quarterback Dave Leggett told WBNS-AM: "Hop's interception broke it wide open. I remember it like it was yesterday."

Wisconsin rallied and had the ball on OSU's 34-yard line when the third quarter ended. As the fourth quarter began, Wisconsin fumbled as Bobo recovered on the OSU 30.

On the first play from scrimmage in the fourth quarter, Cassady broke loose on the right side for a 40-yard pickup. OSU running back Bobby Watkins went eight yards around end to the Wisconsin 22. Watkins then took a short pass from Leggett down to the four. One play later, Bobo powered his way into the end zone for a touchdown. Tad Weed booted his second extra point of the day as Ohio State built a 17-7 lead.

The Badgers went to pieces. On fourth down at its own 39, Wisconsin tried a flat pass that backfired as end Dean Dugger chased Billy Lowe back for a 11-yard loss. The Buckeyes took over on UW's 28. Leggett then faked a pitchout and ran around the Badgers' right side all the way for another touchdown. Following the extra point, OSU led, 24-7.

After the ensuing kickoff, the Badgers' self-destruction continued as they fumbled on an off-tackle play recovered by Ohio State's Don Swartz at UW's 10. One play later, OSU halfback Jerry Harkrader of Middletown scampered in from 10 yards out for a touchdown. Watkins, who sometimes doubled as the placekicker due to substitution rules at that time, booted his second extra point as OSU led, 31-7. Wisconsin would score a final touchdown as the Buckeyes went on to win by a final of 31-14.

Afterward, Cassady was asked by Jack Cowie, *Dispatch* photographer-reporter, to take just one whiff of a rose. Hoppy refused, saying: "It's too early for the smell of roses. When Woody says we smell them, we'll smell them."

Ameche, who would win the 1954 Heisman Trophy, gained only 42 yards on 16 carries. Ameche never scored on the Buckeyes in four seasons. According to Leggett: "Woody always told us heading into the Wisconsin game that if we stopped Ameche, we stop Wisconsin. He had a great knack for picking out the strong and weak points of opponents."

Cassady, who would eventually win the 1955 Heisman, is perhaps the greatest nemesis in the history of Badgers football. Hop's running and catching led the Buckeyes to a 23-14 victory over top-ranked Wisconsin in 1952.

In 1953, with OSU trailing 19-7 going into the final quarter, Cassady won the game on a 60-yard pass play from Leggett as the Buckeyes won in Madison, 20-19. Leggett, subbing for the injured quarterback John Borton turned in what Hayes called a "near perfect game."

In 1955, trailing early, 14-0, Ohio State would go on to win in Madison, 26-16. Cassady led the way with a touchdown and 100 yards rushing in the victory.

The 31-14 victory in 1954 over Wisconsin gave the Buckeyes a 4-0 record in Big Ten play and their first 5-0 start since winning all nine games in 1944. The win over the Badgers established OSU as a national powerhouse once again and would set the scene for a classic showdown later that season at Ohio Stadium against the Michigan Wolverines.

If not for the victory over Wisconsin, the national championship season of 1954 would have never happened. A devastating loss to the second-ranked Badgers could have lead to another loss or two. Leggett says: "Woody always indicated that the '54 team saved his job. Most of those guys were his recruits. People respected him because they figured he knew what he was talking about. He was a great coach and I respected him all of my life."

SCORES BY QUARTERS	1ST	2ND	3RD	4TH	TOTAL
Wisconsin	0	7	0	7	14
Ohio State	0	3	7	21	31

2nd Q-(OSU) Weed 32-yard FG (3-0 OSU)
2nd Q-(WIS) Miller to Levenhagen 33-yd TD (7-3 Wis)
3rd Q-(OSU) Cassady 88-yd int. TD (10-7 OSU)
4th Q-(OSU) Bobo 4-yd TD (17-7 OSU)
4th Q-(OSU) Leggett 28-yd TD (24-7 OSU)
4th Q-(WIS) Gingrass 1-yd TD (24-14 OSU)
4th Q-(OSU) Harkrader 10-yd TD (31-7 OSU)

1955 Rose Bowl

Ohio State 20, USC 7

For only the third time in school history, Ohio State was set to play at the Rose Bowl in Pasadena, California. Following a 9-0 regular season, OSU faced the 8-3 Trojans of USC. The Trojans stumbled into the Rose Bowl having lost the final two games of their season to UCLA and Notre Dame. Ohio State was awarded the 1954 Associated Press national title, while UCLA (9-0) received the same honor from United Press International.

Despite losing to eventual Pacific Coast Conference champion UCLA 34-0, USC was extended an offer to play OSU in the Rose Bow by virtue of the "no-repeat clause" in the conference. The year before, the Bruins had lost in the Rose Bowl to Michigan State, 28-20. Even though the best matchup wasn't to be presented in the Rose Bowl, some 2,000 fans stood in line for up to 20 hours to buy tickets for seats behind the goal line.

On Saturday, December 18, 1954, some 60 OSU players and coaches boarded a DC-7 Mainliner at Port Columbus. The night before in Chicago, crews had painted "Ohio State" on the plane's nose, and by the side door an OSU pennant with the inscription "Rose Bowl Special."

Meanwhile, head coach Woody Hayes's wife, Anne, and nine-year-old son, Steve, made the trip as well. Mary McGarey of the *Columbus Dispatch* wrote: "Steve checked and rechecked his small scarlet traveling bag, balanced a big can of salted almonds under his mother's watchful eye and submitted, reluctantly, to some pictures for photographers."

After arriving in California, Ohio State began the balancing the act of practicing while taking sightseeing tours and participating in several dinners. One of those dinners was held at the Biltmore Hotel in Los Angeles. Comedian Bob Hope, who had spent many years in Cleveland, was the evening's emcee. Hope paraded several Hollywood stars across the stage, including actresses Anita Eckberg and Gloria De Haven. Actor William Holden, comedian Jerry Colonna, and U.S. Chief Justice Earl Warren were also in attendance. Later in the trip, Buckeyes halfback Howard "Hopalong" Cassady met with famed cowboy actor William Boyd from Hennysburg, Ohio, the famed Hopalong Cassidy of the movies.

When Ohio State arrived in California on December 18, the weather for the first couple of days was unseasonably warm with temperatures ranging from the mid-70s to lower 80s. On December 26, Dr. Irving Krick, the meteorologist who had forecasted for the Allies in the Normandy Beach landing some 10 years prior, predicted it was going to rain on New Year's Day. This was something the Rose Bowl had not experienced in the last 30 years in "sunny" California.

Unfortunately, a week later, on New Year's Day, Dr. Krick was correct in his prediction for rain. Besides heavy rain, the fog was so thick that hills and trees in back of the oppo-

site side of the stadium were barely distinguishable. Of the 102,000 tickets sold, the official attendance was only 89,000 due to the inclement weather.

Ohio State won the coin toss and elected to receive. The Buckeyes, who started on their own 29-yard line, mounted an 11-play drive that, after an illegal substitution penalty, ended on the 19. With the ball spotted at the USC 26-yard line, OSU kicker Tad Weed's field goal fell short and wide.

Both teams traded punts before Ohio State's Jim Parker recovered a Trojan fumble at the Buckeyes' 31-yard line. With 3:31 left in the first quarter, the Buckeyes put together the Rose Bowl's first scoring drive of the day. On the second play of the drive, halfback Jerry Harkrader took a pitchout from quarterback Dave Leggett and went 26 yards following fullback Hubert Bobo's block, down to the USC 41-yard line. Later in the drive, Cassady plowed through USC's right tackle for five yards on a fourth and one before the first quarter ended with the score tied at 0-0.

Two plays into the second quarter, Leggett sneaked over right guard for a touchdown. Tad Weed's extra point was good as Ohio State led USC, 7-0. Three plays following OSU's ensuing kickoff, USC fumbled at its own 35-yard line as Leggett recovered the ball for the Buckeyes. Two plays later, Leggett found halfback Bobby Watkins on a 21-yard scoring strike. Tad Weed added his second extra point attempt of the afternoon as OSU built a 14-0 lead over USC.

Later, during the second quarter, USC halfback Aramis Dandoy fielded an OSU punt on his own 14-yard line. Behind great blocking and some dazzling running, Dandoy returned the punt 86 yards for the Trojans' only touchdown of the afternoon. The extra point was good as USC pulled to within a touchdown of the heavily favored Buckeyes at

14-7. The run broke a Rose Bowl record of 61 yards by Billy Wells of Michigan State in the 1954 contest. Neither team was able to score again before halftime as the Buckeyes ran off the field with a seven-point lead.

Covered in mud and soaking wet, Hayes ordered the team to switch to new white jerseys in the locker room. It didn't matter; in the second half their jerseys had changed to a dark brown color, making it difficult for those watching to determine who each player was from both sides.

Late in the third quarter, Ohio State blew a chance to widen the gap to 14 points. On fourth and goal from USC's two-yard line, the Trojans defense held as they stopped OSU's Watkins on a pitchout from Leggett for a two-yard loss, taking over at its own four. On first down, USC's Jon Arnett circled his right end and ran 70 yards to the Ohio State 26 before Cassady pinned him against the sideline as the third quarter ended. Four plays later, the Buckeyes took over on downs at their own 23.

With the Buckeyes clinging to a seven-point lead, Leggett set the wheels in motion for a knockout punch that would secure an Ohio State victory by running 11 yards for a first down to OSU's 34. Five plays later, Leggett faked a pass and rumbled around his right end for 22 more yards down to the Trojans' 28. Cassady then went six yards over right guard followed by Harkrader's one-yard gain. Harkrader gained one more yard, but OSU was offside and penalized to the 26. Following Leggett's two-yard pickup, OSU was faced with a fourth and six from the USC 24.

Having missed from nearly the same range to open the game, Hayes decided to try for the first down. In a heavy downpour, Leggett found Harkrader on a pass play that gained 15 yards down to the Trojan nine. On the very next play, Harkrader took Leggett's pitch into the end zone for a touchdown, culminating in OSU's 11-play, 77-yard drive for a score. Tad Weed's extra point was blocked as OSU settled for a 20-7 lead with 6:41 left in the fourth quarter.

By this time, the rain was coming down in monsoon fashion with the muddy field glistening under the lights. Unfortunately for the sportswriters, serious problems were developing in the open press box. Heavy rains damaged the Western Union circuit wires, preventing many writers from filing their pre-game write-ups. With the rain falling, USC wasn't able to get anything going in the final 6:41 of the contest as Ohio State won by a final score of 20-7. It was the Buckeyes' third Rose Bowl victory in school history.

Leggett was named the game's Most Valuable Player. Running the Split-T, Leggett handed the ball off 80 times in the rain and mud without a fumble. He also rushed for 67 yards and a touchdown while passing for another. Defensively, Leggett intercepted a USC pass. All-American Hopalong Cassady rushed for a team-high 92 yards. Watkins had 64 yards, Harkrader gained 49, while Bobo added another 19 on the ground for a total of 304 rushing yards, only 16 short of the Rose Bowl record.

Ohio State's running attack netted 22 first downs, just two short of the Rose Bowl record set by Georgia against UCLA back in 1943. The Buckeyes rushed for 304 yards, but lost nine for a net of 295.

Afterward in the locker room, the *Columbus Dispatch* reported a soaking wet Hayes stood on top of the white benches and said: "You're the No. 1 team! I said it before and I'll still say it." Hayes then told reporters: "Our kids played good ball" and that they were "about two-touchdown favorites over Southern Cal, maybe a little more." As far as a national championship, Hayes said: "I still think that we're the number-one team in the nation. When you get 19 first downs on a muddy field, that's pretty good going."

Unfortunately for Hayes, a battle with the west coast writers developed on this trip. Before the game, Hayes closed some practices to the writers, something that they were not accustomed to with visiting Rose Bowl teams. Two days before the contest he tried to hide the fact that eight players were sick with food poisoning, saying afterwards to the *Columbus Dispatch*: "I had two reasons for concealing it if possible. I did not want anyone to feel I was setting up an alibi and I did not want anything to get out that might give aid and comfort to the enemy. I wouldn't have told anyone about it, and I told the trainers and physicians to try to keep it quiet."

Hayes was also upset that the field had not been covered before game time despite heavy rain and felt neither school's band should have been allowed to perform on the field at halftime. According to Leggett: "Woody was mad because they didn't cover the field with a tarp before the game and then the people at the Rose Bowl allowed the bands onto the field during halftime. That really chewed things up and made the field even worse than what it had been before. I guess after he told the reporters that after the game, they really gave him heck about that."

In winning the Rose Bowl, the 1954 Buckeyes became the first Ohio State team to ever win 10 games in a season. As far as winning 10 in a row, Hayes shook his head and said: "I suppose you newspapermen would say this is idealistic and doggone, it is. But this game wouldn't be as great as it is—there wouldn't be enough interest to cover it unless it was a great game and a clean game. These were great boys we had on this team this year. They respected each other."

ABOVE: Hubert Bobo (OSU 42), Dean Duggar (OSU 83) and Jim Parker (OSU 62) bring down tailback Jon Arnett (USC 26). (Ohio State University Photo Archive)

While it was an excited and joyous locker room, it was also a locker room filled with players in terrible pain. Nearly all those who played in at least half of the game suffered sand burns. The all-day downpour along with all of the game action and halftime festivities had chewed up the thin turf, bringing the sand to the top. According to Leggett: "It rained the whole game. It was a tough situation. There was so much sand on the field that it worked its way between our tight spandex pants and skin. Several of our players had to go to the hospital because of severe sand burns. Two guys had to spend the night. Hop was allowed to violate a long-standing rule of the

Huntington Hotel dining room on Sunday morning by showing up without a jacket, because his forearms were so raw and sore."

An uncomfortable plane ride awaited the players the next day. Three players, Leggett, center Bob Thornton, and end Dean Dugger, all flew out that night for the Senior Bowl in Mobile, Alabama. Two others, halfback Bobby Watkins and right end Dick Brubaker, left on Sunday for the Hula Bowl in Hawaii, in the company of Cleveland Browns greats Otto Graham and Lou Groza.

Following three lackluster seasons, the 1954 campaign was the turning point in Hayes's coaching career. The Buckeyes became the first Big Ten team since Amos Alonzo Stagg's 1913 Chicago squad (the year Woody was born) to win seven conference games in one season. Ohio State had already been awarded the number one ranking and the mythical national championship by the pollsters before the showdown with USC. The 1955 Rose Bowl victory cemented the Buckeyes' place in history as one of the greatest Ohio State teams ever. They completed their season 10-0 and won Woody's first national championship. The foundation had been laid for years to come.

SCORES BY QUARTER	1ST	2ND	3RD	4TH	TOTAL
Ohio State	0	14	0	6	20
USC	0	7	0	0	7

2nd Q-(OSU) Leggett 3-yard TD (7-0 OSU)
2nd Q-(OSU) Leggett to Watkins 21-yd TD (14-0 OSU)
2nd Q-(USC) Dandoy 86-yd punt return TD (14-7 OSU)
4th Q-(OSU) Harkrader 9-yd TD (Extra point failed, 20-7 OSU)

ABOVE: The OSU backfield poses for pictures prior to the Rose Bowl. From left: Hubert Bobo (42), Bobby Watkins (45), Dave Leggett (22) and Hopalong Cassady (40). (Ohio State University Photo Archive)

1950 SNOW BOWL

MICHIGAN 9, OHIO STATE 3

BONUS GAME

You've heard the phase "right place, right time?" In March of 2003, the *Buckeye Sports Bulletin* ran an article about a local radio series I host during the summer months called "Buckeye Glory Days." Ohio State football historian and good friend Jack Park and I host a 10-game series on past Ohio State football games on WBNS-AM, Columbus, Ohio. When asked by BSB editor Frank Moskowitz about the series, I told him I was always looking for games taped off the radio prior to 1974, and if anyone had a copy, to please call me.

About a month later, a man by the name of Larry Brunk from Elida, Ohio, wrote me a letter. He had a copy of the 1950 Ohio State-Michigan game. Larry wanted to know if I would like a copy of the broadcast. I immediately called him back to ask how he obtained a copy of the game. Larry's response was: "I was seven years old and decided to tape the game on my new reel-to-reel machine because my father and grandfather were going to the game. I didn't have much tape, so I turned it off between plays, but I have most of the contest." After speaking awhile longer to Larry, I asked him to mail it to me so I could make a copy of the only known taped radio broadcast of the game still in existence.

In August of 2003, what we had of the 1950 "Snow Bowl" aired on "Buckeye Glory Days." Longtime voice of the Ohio State Buckeyes Marv Homan joined Jack and me in the studio for two hours of great memories. Now in his early 80s, Homan is as spry as he

was some 53 years earlier on the day of the original broadcast. He winced and shook his head from time to time listening to a young radio announcer making rookie mistakes. All the while the listening audience was mesmerized at the exploits being relived on the air during those terrible weather conditions on November 25, 1950.

When I originally ran this book idea past various members of the panel, they each said: "The Snow Bowl has to be number one." Remember, this was before the Buckeyes' perfect season of 2002 or before I even knew a tape existed of the 1950 OSU-UM game. I informed the panel that I had decided to revisit the last 50 years, starting in 1954, not knowing that I would be lucky enough to find "Snow Bowl" audio. By then, it was too late to change the book. Instead, I decided to give the 1950 Ohio State-Michigan contest its own special chapter. After reading the book, I think that you, the readers, should decide where to place this historic game.

Imagine it's the Friday prior to the 1950 Ohio State-Michigan football game. The weatherman calls for a chance of light snow, high in the 30s with temperatures falling on Saturday. Not too bad; most fans could deal with that. Instead, without warning, a blizzard develops the next morning. That's what Ohio State fans and players faced heading out to the biggest game of the year. The winds picked up to 40 miles per hour as the temperatures steadily dropped into the teens. The snow, driven by strong winds, began to pile up one

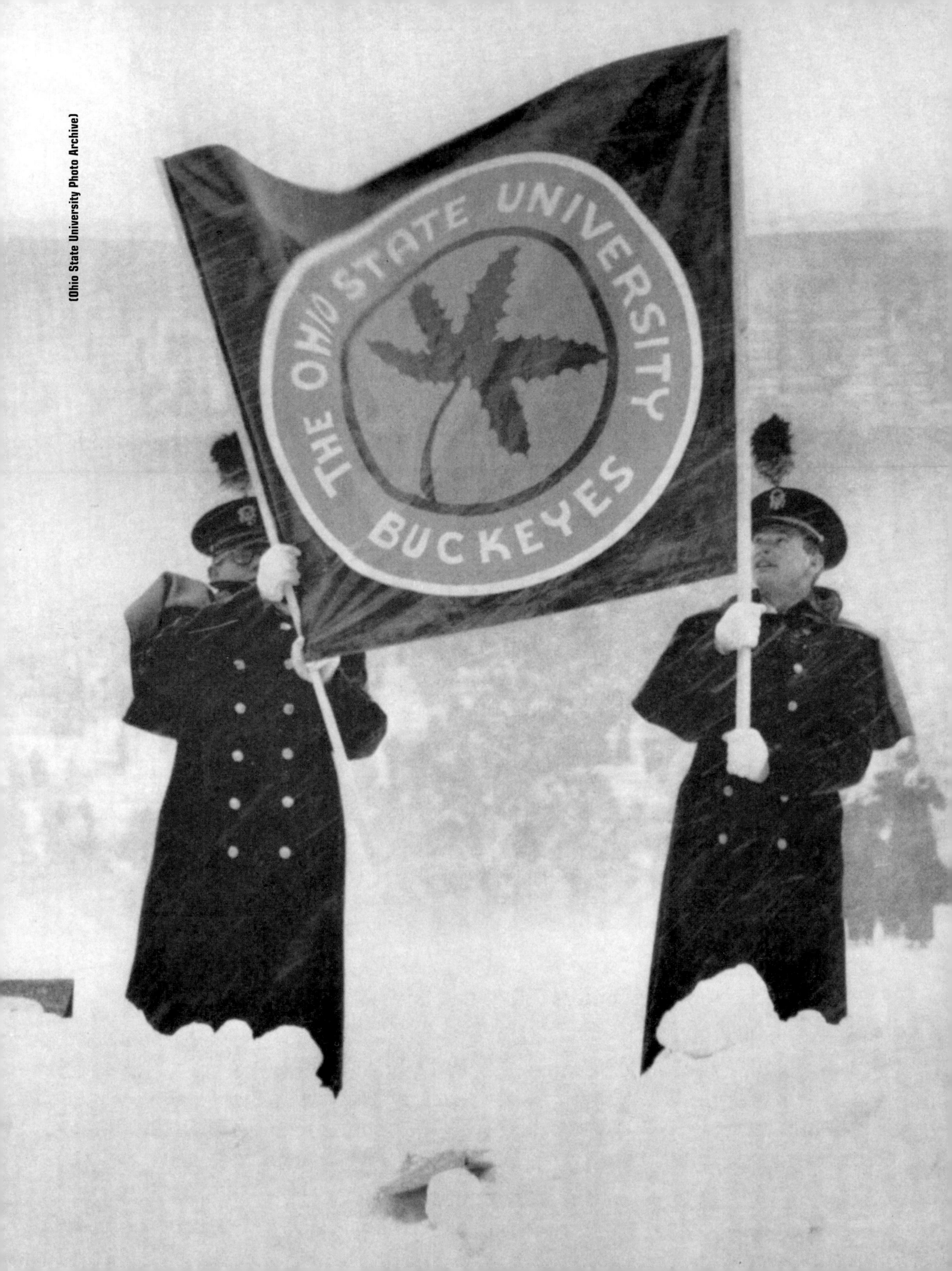

(Ohio State University Photo Archive)

to two feet in some spots. Fans began to trickle into Ohio Stadium. The start of the game was delayed 20 minutes as members of the grounds crew and fans tried to remove the tarp from the field. With the conditions deteriorating rapidly, crews were only able to remove tarps covering one half of the field. The other tarp was frozen onto the playing surface, where it remained for the game.

At a meeting upstairs in the stadium tower, Ohio State athletic director Dick Larkins wanted to postpone the contest until the following Saturday due to the dangerous and unplayable conditions on the field. An effort was made twice to contact Big Ten commissioner Tug Wilson, who was attending another game and unavailable. The late Paul Hornung of the *Columbus Dispatch* wrote: "Michigan Athletic Director Fritz Crisler told Larkins: 'We're here now. We're not coming back.'" When OSU Coach Wes Fesler found out that the game would go on as scheduled, he protested, saying: "This is crazy!"

It was an important matchup for Ohio State. The Buckeyes were 5-1 in league play. Michigan was 3-1-1. An Ohio State victory over Michigan would give the Buckeyes their second straight Big Ten title. But because of the no-repeat policy at that time, OSU could not return to the Rose Bowl. If the Wolverines upset Ohio State and Illinois beat Northwestern, the Illini would play in Pasadena, California on New Years Day.

A reported 50,503 die-hard fans showed up to watch the November 25, 1950 matchup between Ohio State and Michigan. Many huddled under B deck. Some didn't move downstairs but remained in the seats they had purchased in C deck. The snow fell horizontally, driven by winds clocked at 40 miles per hour. The snow, which was falling more heavily now, stung the faces of those in attendance while frostbite was on the minds of everyone.

An 18-year-old OSU student, who would later become an assistant coach under future head coach Woody Hayes and eventually the man who replaced Hayes as head coach, Earle Bruce, watched the game by himself in A deck: "I'll go back to the Wednesday leading up to the game where tickets were going for $75.00 apiece. That was a lot of money back then. Someone said to hold onto them, don't sell them, you'll get $150.00 per ticket by Friday. Well, Friday night came and it started snowing and it snowed and it snowed and it snowed. On Saturday, you could hardly get down High Street, much less the rest of town, due to the fact we had something like 15 to 20 inches of snow eventually over the weekend. Not only heavy snow, but also strong winds. It was a blizzard. The ground crew swept the field as best they could to find the yard lines.

"It shouldn't have been played. Well, they play the game, although it wasn't fit to play. Some people say that football is football, but it was a great equalizer for Michigan. They won the game and rightly so because they didn't make the mistakes that we made. It was so bad that the snow piled up about at least three to four feet deep on each sideline. Conditions were as bad as I've ever seen on a football field. I've never seen a game like that before or since."

In the first quarter, Ohio State defensive lineman Bob Momsen blocked a Wolverines punt, which the Buckeyes recovered deep in Michigan territory. The maize and blue then held Ohio State on the next three downs. Coach Fesler then called for a field goal attempt. All-America halfback Vic Janowicz grabbed a broom from an official and cleared out a spot at the 28-yard line. Fans strained to watch Janowicz's 38-yard attempt into the north end of the field. By now, it was snowing so hard that fans in the west stands could barely see those sitting in the east stands and vice versa. Janowicz lined up and kicked a 38-yard field goal to give Ohio State a 3-0 lead. To this day, those who saw Janowicz make the field goal would still say it's one of the most remarkable feats in college football history.

Late in the first quarter, Janowicz tried to punt from his end zone, only to have it blocked out of bounds for a safety. Michigan was now on the scoreboard and trailed Ohio State by a score of 3-2. With only 47 seconds remaining before halftime, one of the most infamous moves in OSU football history took place. Following another Michigan punt the Buckeyes were again backed up on their own goal line. Two running plays failed and Fesler sent in the punt team.

Meanwhile, Bruce, who was sitting in the lower deck on the west side, watched in amazement at what was about to take place: "I was sitting behind this 80-year-old lady who realized, before anyone else, what Coach Fesler was going to do next. When Janowicz came in on third down, the little old lady stood up and yelled 'Don't you dare punt! Don't you dare punt, Fesler!' Sure enough, on third down, Janowicz attempted a punt, which Michigan then blocked and recovered for the only touchdown of the day. It was a terrible way to lose, and that old lady knew before anyone what was going to happen."

The ironic thing about the blocked punt was that Tony Momsen of Michigan happened to be the one who recovered the ball in the end zone for the touchdown. He was the younger brother of Ohio State's Bob Momsen, who had blocked a Michigan punt early in the first quarter. Michigan converted the extra point as the half ended with the Wolverines leading, 9-3. Neither team could score in the second half as Michigan ruined Ohio State's chances of an outright Big Ten championship by winning the "Snow Bowl" at Ohio Stadium.

The two teams combined for 45 total punts, with Janowicz booting 21 that afternoon for a total of 685 yards. Michigan quarterback Chuck Ortman punted the ball 24 times for 723 yards. The Wolverines won the contest despite not making a first down. All of the points were scored as a result of blocked punts. The two teams combined for 10 fumbles on the day. Michigan had six and Ohio State four and each lost only one.

According to former WOSU-AM announcer Marv Homan: "After the game, officials went through the stands looking to make sure no one had succumbed to the conditions. It would have been easy for someone who had too much to drink to pass out and get covered up by the snow. No one would have noticed for a few days. It was scary and they were very concerned about that."

A few weeks later, Janowicz was named the winner of the Heisman Trophy. Meanwhile, Fesler unexpectedly resigned. In the aftermath of the loss to Michigan, Fesler, a three time All-America end at Ohio State (1928-30) caught incredible heat from his critics. Despite horrible weather conditions, a loss to the Wolverines was unacceptable. Fesler resigned on December 9, 1950, with a 0-3-1 record against Michigan. The "graveyard of coaches" continued in Columbus. On February 18, 1951, a little known coach named Woody Hayes would take over and proceed to go 16-11-1 the next 28 seasons against the Wolverines. Sometimes, things do work out for the best.

SCORES BY QUARTERS	1ST	2ND	3RD	4TH	TOTAL
Michigan	2	7	0	0	9
Ohio State	3	0	0	0	3

1st Q-(OSU) Janowicz 38-yd FG (3-0 OSU)
1st Q-(UM) Wahl blocks a Janowicz punt out of the end zone for a safety (3-2 OSU)
2nd Q-(UM) Allis recovers a blocked Janowicz punt in the end zone for a TD (9-3 UM)

1974 ROSE BOWL

OHIO STATE 42, USC 21

In the 1970s, the Big Ten Conference was known as "The Big Two and the Little Eight," and for good reason. The only two schools in the conference to represent the Big Ten in the Rose Bowl were Ohio State and Michigan. As Bo Schembechler at Michigan put it: "When I was hired by Michigan in December of 1968, I was set to beat one and only one team. I only wanted Ohio State. That's the team I wanted to beat. Michigan could beat those other guys, but Ohio State was different. So I talked about it all the time and I did something every day to beat Ohio State and to beat Woody. He did the same thing with me in Columbus. Remember, I worked for him for five years and knew him. Michigan consumed him as Ohio State did me."

In 1970, OSU defeated Michigan, 20-9, only to lose to Stanford. The following season, Michigan won the Big Ten as they defeated Ohio State, then lost to USC. In 1972, Ohio State's defense provided goal line stands on two occasions, beating Michigan, 14-11, before getting crushed by USC in the Rose Bowl. The 42-17 shellacking by the Trojans gave Ohio State the inspiration they needed to prove themselves the next season, much like the defeat at Michigan in 1969 had done for the 1970 squad.

Ohio State had earned the right to play in the 1974 Rose Bowl despite a season-ending 10-10 tie at Michigan. With both teams tying for the conference champi-onship at 7-0-1, the conference athletic directors would vote the following day in Chicago to see which team would represent the conference in Pasadena.

Wolverines quarterback Dennis Franklin separated his shoulder in the tie, but Schembechler was confident that the conference athletic directors would vote to have the Wolverines play on New Year's Day. Most felt that with Michigan tying then top-ranked Ohio State and both ending up at 7-0-1 in conference play, the vote would go the Wolverines' way. To the surprise of almost everyone, the Buckeyes were selected to represent the Big Ten conference. The *Detroit Free Press* reported the vote as 6-4 in favor of Ohio State. Schembechler called it "tragic" upon hearing the news and later said that he would "never forgive those who voted against his team."

The good news was totally unexpected and obviously welcomed at Ohio State. It would be a chance to show the nation why they had been the top-ranked team in the country for eight weeks before dropping to third following the tie at Michigan. It was also a chance to avenge their 42-17 loss to USC in the 1973 Rose Bowl.

All-America tackle John Hicks was asked 30 years later if he remembered what he was doing the day of the vote. "I was with Coach Hayes. He was telling me that the conference always favored Michigan and that was the last game he was going to coach with me and we were spending a little time

ABOVE: OSU fullback Pete Johnson (33) dives for a touchdown. USC defensive lineman Gary Jeter (79) runs in hot pursuit. (Ohio State University Photo Archive)

reflecting. We had a great five years together. I recently saw Bo at the Hall of Fame in 2001 and he's still bitter about that vote. He said that he got cheated. I said to him, 'Coach, I got the films, do you want me to send them to you?' He laughed, but I don't think that he thought it was very funny."

Ohio State's defense entered the Rose Bowl ranked number one in the country, having allowed only 43 points in ten games. Four of the Buckeyes' nine victories were shutouts. Two of the wins saw OSU allow only three points apiece while two teams scored just seven points. Quarterback Pat Hayden, receiver Lynn Swann and tailback Anthony Davis led USC's powerful offensive unit.

USC opened up the game by hitting four consecutive passes before stalling on the Ohio State 30-yard line. Chris Limahelu then connected on a 47-yard field goal that broke the USC record and was the second longest in Rose Bowl history, giving the Trojans a 3-0 lead. Ohio State's Cornelius Green then served up an interception on the Buckeyes' 41-yard line. USC's next attempt at a field goal went wide right from 47 yards out.

Ohio State's first big break came late in the first quarter after Southern Cal was called for offsides on Blair Conway's 36-yard field goal attempt. The Buckeyes then went for it on fourth down as Archie Griffin went for 13 yards and a first down. Two plays later, big Pete

"Coach Hayes had a few choice words for us after SC made it 21-14. Then he challenged the offense to go back in and get the touchdown back, which they did."

—Randy Gradishar

Johnson bowled his way into the end zone for a touchdown. Conway's extra point was good and Ohio State grabbed their first lead of the game at 7-3.

In the second quarter, USC hit a 42-yard field goal before going ahead on receiver J.K. McKay's (son of USC head coach John McKay) touchdown pass to running back Anthony Davis. Pat Hayden then hit McKay on a two-point conversion as USC led the Buckeyes at 14-7. Ohio State charged right back with a 12-play drive. Freshman fullback Pete Johnson powered his way over right tackle John Hicks to score his second touchdown of the afternoon. Conway connected on his second extra point as Ohio State tied USC at 14 all.

In the third quarter, with Ohio State driving, USC recovered an Archie Griffin fumble at their own 16-yard line. The Trojans then put together a 14-play, 84-yard drive to take the lead as Anthony Davis scored from one yard out. Limahelu converted the extra point for a 21-14 USC lead. The vaunted Ohio State defense, which had given up only 43 points in ten previous games, had already given up 21 with a quarter and a half to play. Some 30 years later, Randy Gradishar would tell WBNS-AM: "Coach Hayes had a few choice words for us after SC made it 21-14. Then, he challenged the offense to go back in and get the touchdown back, which they did."

After taking the ensuing kickoff, the Buckeyes were flagged for holding back to their own 21-yard line. Following the miscue,

the Buckeyes put together a lightening-quick drive. Greene ran for 16 yards up to the OSU 37-yard line, but received 15 more yards as USC was flagged for a late tackle, which moved the ball to the Trojans' 48-yard line. Greene then found tight end Fred Pagac on a 39-yard pass down to the USC four-yard line. On the next play, Johnson ran through a gaping hole into the end zone for a touchdown. Conway's extra point attempt was blocked and the Buckeyes trailed 21-20 with 4:53 left in the third quarter.

Late in the third quarter, the OSU defense finally stiffened, forcing USC to punt. Ohio State defensive back Neil Colzie turned the game around, taking the Trojans' punt 56 yards. This set up Greene's short touchdown run. This time Conway's extra point attempt was good and the Buckeyes led, 27-21.

In the fourth quarter, OSU scored again with fullback Bruce Elia, who punched the ball over from one yard out. The Buckeyes went for two as Corny Green ran it in and the Buckeyes' lead was now 35-21. With less than five minutes remaining, super sophomore Archie Griffin got into the scoring act as he scampered 47 yards for a touchdown. It was the icing on the cake Ohio State was looking for as they built an insurmountable 42-21 lead following Conway's conversion of the extra point.

The 42-21 victory over USC ended a string of four straight Big Ten losses to Pac-8 teams. For the 60-year-old Hayes, his record at Ohio State improved to 159-49-8, including a

4-2 mark at the Rose Bowl. Afterward, Coach Hayes told the *Columbus Dispatch* along with the assembled media: "The greatest victory I ever had. It may be the greatest victory we ever had. We had some that didn't lose any, but didn't tie either. It's difficult to say. They were the greatest team today. We have never been this good in the Rose Bowl."

Ohio State's offense dominated USC's defense, rolling up 449 total yards, 320 of those coming on the ground. Archie Griffin led all rushers with 149 yards, including a 47-yard touchdown run late in the fourth quarter. Freshman fullback Pete Johnson rushed 21 times for 94 yards and three touchdowns while quarterback Corny Greene along with fullback Bruce Elia each scored touchdowns as well. Green's touchdown came after Neil Colzie returned a punt 56 yards.

Before the Rose Bowl, reporters kept asking Hayes if the Buckeyes would have to pass it more to beat USC. Woody responded, "Oh, I agree," but then he went on to say: "We're not a passing team; let's not joke about it." Six weeks prior, in the 10-10 tie at Michigan, Ohio State never threw a pass until it was too late. Everyone knew that Woody was conservative on offense, but for most, the brutally conservative offense was a hard pill to swallow. Later, everyone found out why. Greene's right thumb was badly swollen after he jammed it in the win over Iowa a week prior to the Michigan contest. In the Rose Bowl, Greene's first pass was intercepted before he completed seven of the next eight passes for 129 yards. Outside of the interception, all seven completions were key plays. Greene's outstanding play earned him the game's Most Valuable Player Award.

Senior tight end Fred Pagac had his biggest day as a Buckeye, catching four passes for 89 yards. Pagac, who would later play in the NFL for the Chicago Bears, would also become OSU's assistant head coach before moving on to the coaching ranks of the NFL.

Griffin, the winner of the 1974 and 1975 Heisman Trophy awards, would go on to play one more season for Ohio State before being drafted by the Cincinnati Bengals, where he played for eight seasons. Upon retiring, Griffin returned to OSU as an associate director of athletics. Griffin, who is now in charge of the Ohio State Alumni Association, reflected back on that game some 30 years later by saying: "That 42-17 loss to USC in the 1973 Rose Bowl was our inspiration going into the 1974 Rose Bowl game. In 1973, we had a great team that went undefeated, but did tie Michigan. The Big Ten athletic directors had to vote between Ohio State and Michigan to go to Pasadena. Many people wanted Michigan to go since we had been beaten so bad the year before. But they voted for us and we went out there and really surprised some people, because they didn't think that we could do that. So that was sweet revenge for us that season."

SCORES BY QUARTERS	1ST	2ND	3RD	4TH	TOTAL
Ohio State	7	7	13	15	42
USC	3	11	7	0	21

1st Q-(USC) Limahelu 47-yd FG (3-0 USC)
1st Q-(OSU) Johnson 1-yd TD (7-3 OSU)
2nd Q-(USC) Limahelu 42-yd FG (7-6 OSU)
2nd Q-(USC) Davis 10-yd TD pass to McKay (USC 2-pt conversion good, Hayden to McKay, 14-7 USC)
2nd Q-(OSU) Johnson 1-yd TD (14-14)
3rd Q-(USC) Davis 1-yd TD (21-14 USC)
3rd Q-(OSU) Johnson 4-yd TD (Extra Point missed by Conway-21-20 USC)
3rd Q-(OSU) Greene 1-yd TD (27-21 OSU)
4th Q-(OSU) Elia 2-yd TD (OSU 2-point conversion good, Greene runs it in for two-point conversion 35-21 OSU)
4th Q-(OSU) Griffin 47-yd TD (42-21 OSU)

1970

OHIO STATE 20, MICHIGAN 9

In 1970, the longest winter in Columbus history ended in April with the start of spring practice. Four painful months had passed since the unexpected loss at Michigan on November 22, 1969. The biggest revenge game in Ohio State history would take place in November at Ohio Stadium against the Wolverines. Head coach Woody Hayes had already begun his psychology with his players. A large white rug bearing the score of the 24–12 loss to the Wolverines was placed on the floor of the entrance of the locker room. It would serve as a constant reminder of what happened and what the Buckeyes must do to achieve their primary goal: BEAT MICHIGAN!

The super sophomores of 1968 were now seniors. This senior class had gone 18-1, having won the national championship following its New Year's Day Rose Bowl victory of 1969 over USC. The loss at Ann Arbor in November of 1969 served as a wake-up call. The seemingly unbeatable Buckeyes were fallible, and they didn't want a repeat of their subpar performance.

While not as dominating offensively as they had been in 1969, Ohio State rolled through its first four games with wins over Texas A&M, Duke, Michigan State and Minnesota. On October 24, OSU trailed

Illinois in Champaign 23-16 early in the third quarter before pulling out a 48-29 victory over the Illini. OSU then slipped past Northwestern 24-10 before winning at Wisconsin and Purdue. OSU defeated the Boilermakers 10-7 on Fred Schram's tie-breaking field goal, which set up a season-ending home date with Michigan.

The 25th title-bearing meeting between Ohio State and Michigan was set for November 21, 1970. OSU entered the contest 8-0 overall and ranked fourth in the coaches' poll. The Wolverines were fifth nationally at 8-0. The rankings were reversed in the writers Associated Press poll. It marked the first time since 1905 when Chicago beat Michigan 2-0 that conference teams had gone into the title game with perfect records. The Big Ten championship and a trip to the Rose Bowl hung in the balance for Ohio State. With the Big Ten still adhering to the "no repeat rule" for the Rose Bowl, a Big Ten title, a win over OSU and an undefeated season was what Michigan was looking to accomplish.

The state of Ohio was at a fever pitch. "Beat Michigan" bumper sticker mania was at an all-time high around Columbus. "There ain't no bumper stickers that ever won a game, or for that matter, ever elected a candidate," Bo Schembechler snickered. For Coach

OPPOSITE: OSU linebacker Stan White (88) made the key interception to turn the game against UM. (Brockway Sports Photos)

Hayes, it was more than a trip to Pasadena and another Big Ten title, it was a chance to exact revenge against his former pupil who had beaten him the year before.

On November 22, 1970, a record crowd of 87,331 packed Ohio Stadium nearly an hour before game time to watch the fifth-ranked Buckeyes and the fourth-ranked Wolverines. Not only was there a record number of fans at the Horseshoe, there were also 619 writers and sportscasters on hand as well.

The anticipation, for both the fans and the teams, was almost unbearable. Michigan's nerves were tested first as OSU's Harry Howard recovered Lance Scheffler's fumble on the opening kickoff. The Buckeyes then grabbed a 3-0 lead on Fred Schram's 28-yard field goal with 12:18 to go in the first quarter. Following a Kern interception, Michigan was able to set up a Dana Coin 31-yard field goal that tied the score early in the second quarter, 3-3.

The Buckeyes took the lead again right before halftime thanks to a costly mistake by Michigan. The Wolverines' Paul Staroba had nailed a 72-yard punt that was nullified by a facemask penalty. Tim Anderson returned Staroba's second punt to the OSU 47-yard line. Quarterback Rex Kern then led OSU on a 53-yard, 10-play drive, which culminated in a perfectly thrown 26-yard touchdown pass to split end Bruce Jankowski. Schram's extra point was good and Ohio State led Michigan 10-3 in a hard-fought first half of play.

Late in the second quarter, OSU linebacker Stan White, who would play a significant role later in the game, recovered a Wolverines fumble on the Michigan 46-yard line. Following a 19-yard pass from Kern to Tom Campana and a two-yard run by Hayden, Hayes sent Schram onto the field.

But Kern sent Schram back to the sidelines. Hayes memorably sent Schram back again before Kern called time to confer with Hayes. With 22 seconds remaining in the first half, the coach wanted to attempt a field goal. Kern told Hayes that he could run one more play and still have time for a field goal attempt. Kern got his wish and completed a short pass to Brockington at the Michigan 19-yard line, but the play ended inbounds and time ran out before another play could be started. Hayes later said he regretted not sticking to his original choice.

Ohio State was forced to punt to open up the third quarter after its drive stalled. Michigan took over at midfield and marched down the field with quarterback Don Moorehead hitting Staroba on a 13-yard touchdown pass. The extra point was no good and Ohio State's lead was 10-9. Almost the entire third quarter was played in Ohio State territory. Michigan's defense held the Buckeyes without a first down on the next two drives, forcing punts.

Early in the fourth quarter, still leading 10-9, Ohio State's offense finally got into gear with Hayes going back to his bread and butter. The running attack began to show its muscle. OSU ran the ball 10 straight times before Kern found end Jan White on a 16-yard pass play to Michigan's 11-yard line. Kern then missed White in the end zone, forcing Schram to boot a 27-yard field goal. The field goal gave the Buckeyes some breathing room at 13-9 with 10:57 left in the game.

The deciding play of the game came on the next series. On third and 13, Ohio State linebacker Stan White picked off a Moorehead pass at Michigan's 23-yard line before returning it down to Michigan's nine-yard line. White later would tell WBNS-AM in 2003: "I

"I've got to feel this was our greatest victory. This makes up for what happened last year!"

—Coach Woody Hayes

always tell everybody that was the one play—and I was lucky enough to play 13 years of pro ball—of all the years, that's the only play where I remember hearing the crowd in the middle of a play. As the ball was about five yards away from me, I guess everybody could see that I was going to intercept it and they just erupted into what can only happen at Ohio Stadium. It was just a tremendous roar, the only time I can actually remember hearing a crowd during a play."

Going for the jugular, OSU went back to its ground attack as Brockington carried the ball for a yard. Kern, on a keeper, picked up four more yards down to the four-yard line. The stadium was electric with anticipation and the Buckeyes were ready to deliver a knockout blow. On third and goal from the Wolverines' four-yard line, Kern ran wide right, keeping the Michigan defenders guessing until the final instant, then pitched the ball wide to Hayden, who walked into the end zone. Schram's extra point was good as Ohio State increased its lead to 20-9.

Late in the contest, Rick Galbos exploded for a 32-yard gain, the longest of the afternoon, as Ohio State positioned itself for another touchdown. Time ran out before the Buckeyes could score again as the fans swarmed onto the field, ripping the goal posts, concrete and all, out of the ground in celebration. According to postgame reports in the

Columbus Dispatch, Hayes came off the field clutching a football. Most of the team had already followed Governor James Rhodes off the field into the locker room where they sang: "We don't give a damn for the whole state of Michigan… We're from O-H-I-O." Meanwhile, Hayes posed for pictures after the game in the locker room, with a finger raised in a "We're No. 1 signal," unprecedented for him. Hayes also received a postgame call from his old friend, President Nixon, who offered his congratulations.

With the press literally jammed into the postgame meeting area, Hayes was asked whether he thought his Buckeyes deserved to be rated number one. Woody's answer: "You're damn right I do!" Hayes went on to tell the *Dispatch* and several hundred other papers, "I've got to feel this was our greatest victory. This makes up for what happened last year! This justifies in the minds of our seniors that they are the greatest group of players we ever had here, having won 27 of 28 games."

In the 20-9 victory over Michigan, Ohio State did two things effectively. They rushed the ball for 242 yards while defensively giving up only 37 yards on the ground to the Wolverines. OSU halfback Leo Hayden led the Buckeyes with 28 carries for 117 yards and a touchdown, many of those yards coming on a delay-type play. Hayes responded with a warfare football analogy:

"It's a funny thing, the Japanese got their plan for attacking Pearl Harbor from our own Fleet Problem No. 14 of 1934. The Germans got the tank from the British. Guess where we got that play? It's in my book [*Hot Line to Victory*] and I got it originally from the fellow at Oklahoma [Chuck Fairbanks]. But Michigan refined it. I saw it in their highlight films and we bought a copy for $80, so we borrowed it back. I'm totally grateful. I truly relish turning an opponent's play against him."

Meanwhile, Brockington, who had carried the ball 27 times for 79 yards, established a new single-season rushing record of 1,040 yards. In 2002, Brockington underwent a life-saving kidney transplant. During the fall of 2003, Brockington came back to Columbus for a fundraiser benefiting the American Kidney Foundation. He recalled how big the victory in 1970 over Michigan really was: "It was huge. You know we lost the year before and we had to walk across that carpet all spring, all summer, and after that Purdue game, we didn't even watch the postgame films of the win over the Boilermakers. I mean Woody went right into that Michigan game and he made us sign papers and put down what we were going to do to beat Michigan. Then he read them all to the team. That's how intense that game was. I mean we could not lose that football game. That was not in the agenda, no way. You had to win it one way or another."

Some 35 years later, I asked Kern which was better: "Winning the national championship or the 1970 over Michigan?" Kern responded: "I've never had that asked. My response is beating Michigan is a lot better than beating SC in the Rose Bowl, even though that was for the national championship. Our focus and goal was always the Big Ten championship and that Rose Bowl goes through that school up north. That was our focus and our goal and when we did that here, it was great!"

It was the final home game at Ohio Stadium for 29 seniors, including two-time All-America middle guard Jim Stillwagon. In 1970, "Wagon," would win the Lombardi Award and was selected Ohio State's Most Valuable Player. Stillwagon remembered the intensity of his final home game by saying: " I came off the field a little limpy, and Coach said, 'Dammit, Jim, you can't get hurt today. You cannot get hurt today.' I turned around and went back onto the field. That's how big it was. We had to make that sacrifice one more time, and fortunately we won 20-9—and went to the Rose Bowl and messed up."

In the Michigan locker room, the loss was as devastating for them as it had been for the Ohio State players the year prior. Schembechler, in a hushed voice, said: "We have nothing to be ashamed of. You have to give credit to Ohio State. They are the best team we've played this year. No question about it."

The 1970 victory over Michigan goes down as one of the greatest of all time. If not for a loss in the New Year's Day Rose Bowl, 27-17 to Stanford, Ohio State would have captured their second national championship in three years. For Kern, a 27-2 record over two years was a great achievement, but not as great as it could have been. "Those two mistakes cost us an unprecedented three national championships. Nobody's ever done that. We were so close to doing that and the loss to Michigan in 1969 our junior year was devastating. When you think back as a player, okay, I've got one more year, how do we correct that for the following year? Well, we did that through the Big Ten conference until we got to Stanford in the 1971 Rose Bowl and it happened again."

ABOVE: To remind players of the '69 loss to Michigan, Hayes designed a rug they had to walk over every day for the next year. (Ohio State University Photo Archive)

The victory over Michigan will go down as one of the greatest games in Ohio State history for several reasons. It avenged the horrible loss the year before at Michigan. It also provided Coach Hayes some comfort in ruining Michigan's perfect season while beating his protégé, Bo Schembechler. Finally, it gave Ohio State an undisputed Big Ten championship, a 9-0 record, and a trip to the Rose Bowl.

SCORES BY QUARTER	1ST	2ND	3RD	4TH	TOTAL
Michigan	0	3	6	0	9
Ohio State	3	7	0	10	20

1st Q-(OSU) Schram 28-yd FG (3-0 OSU)
2nd Q-(UM) Coin 31-yd FG (3-3)
2nd Q-(OSU) Kern to Jankowski 26-yd TD pass (10-3 OSU)
3rd Q-(UM) Moorehead to Staroba 13-yd TD pass (Ex. Point failed 10-9 OSU)
4th Q-(OSU) Schram 27-yd FG (13-9 OSU)
4th Q-(OSU) Hayden 4-yd TD (20-9 OSU)

1977

OKLAHOMA 29, OHIO STATE 28

One of the most highly anticipated games in Ohio State history occurred on September 24, 1977, when the Buckeyes hosted Oklahoma in a non-conference showdown. The anticipation and build-up between these two giants of the college gridiron rivaled the Buckeyes' two-game series against Notre Dame back in 1935-36. It would be the biggest game prior to the start of the Big Ten season in head coach Woody Hayes's 27 years at Ohio State. Both teams were 2-0 heading into the match-up, ranked third and fourth interchangeably in both polls.

Since taking over back in 1951, Hayes had led Ohio State to a 191-54-9 record while winning three national championships and 12 Big Ten titles, the last five in a row. Hayes had only two losing seasons with OSU and was third in college football history with 224 wins, 191 of those coming at Ohio State. During the past five seasons, including the first two games of the 1977 season, OSU had gone an impressive 51-6-2.

Oklahoma's record over nearly that same time span was practically the same. The Sooners' rise to fame began in 1947 under Bud Wilkerson, who in 17 seasons would go 145-29-4. Oklahoma would win three national titles under the direction of Wilkerson in 1950, 1955 and 1956. Following a three-year drop-off following Wilkerson's departure for politics, Oklahoma rebounded under Chuck Fairbanks. He would go 48-18-1 in seven seasons before

leaving to become the head coach of the New England Patriots. Longtime assistant Barry Switzer took over in 1973 and in three seasons won at a phenomenal .895 clip (43-3-2), including back-to-back national titles in 1974 and 1975.

The Sooners' wishbone offense entered the matchup with probably the finest backfield that an Ohio State defense had ever faced. Leading the way at halfback were Elvis Peacock and future Heisman Trophy winner Billy Simms. Kenny King started at fullback while quarterback Thomas Lott directed the Sooners' offense. Oklahoma returned 19 starters, nine of whom were on defense. In the two games leading up to the Ohio State contest, the Sooners had given up a surprising total of 47 points in victories over Vanderbilt and Utah.

Ohio State had opened its season at home with a costly 10-0 victory over the Miami Hurricanes as senior fullback Jeff Logan, along with reserve tailback Ricky Johnson, went down with various leg injuries. To compensate for the injuries, Hayes shifted starting running back Ron Springs to fullback while moving safety Ray Griffin to the starting running back position. For Griffin, it was the same position he played in a limited role during his freshman season before switching to safety, a spot in which he excelled. The following week OSU rolled up 518 yards of total offense in a 38-7 win over the Gophers. The moves worked, as the Buckeyes rushed for 385 yards. Griffin rush-

ABOVE: OSU safety Todd Bell (25) just misses blocking Oklahoma kicker Uwe von Schamann's game-winning 41-yard field goal. (Brockway Sports Photos)

ing for 58 yards on 14 carries, while Springs carried the ball 27 times for 147 yards, both collegiate highs. Defensively, All–America linebacker Tom Cousineau led the defense with 15 tackles, the only points given up on a 100-yard kickoff return. In two games, the OSU defense had yet to allow a point on the board.

Heading into the contest, Hayes was quoted in the *Columbus Dispatch* as saying: "I don't think there is any question that this is an extremely important game. Certainly any time a team with as impressive a record as Oklahoma has had over the last 25 years come to town, it takes on a air of importance. They don't have any trouble getting up for a game like this, but we don't want them to peak early. That's an easy thing to have happen in a game of this type."

The third largest crowd in Ohio Stadium history, 88,119 fans, packed into the Horseshoe on September 24, 1977, for the colossal first-ever showdown between Ohio State and Oklahoma. After months of build-up to the game, the Buckeyes laid a big egg in the opening quarter, falling behind early 20-0. The Sooners opened the game with a six-play, 61-yard touchdown drive with Peacock taking Lott's fumble 33-yards for a touchdown. The extra point was good and Oklahoma led, 7-0.

On the Buckeyes' first play from scrimmage, the Sooners recovered quarterback Rod Gerald's fumble at the OSU 17-yard line. Things quickly went from bad to worse as Ohio State star linebacker Tom Cousineau went down with a separated shoulder and was lost for the rest of the game. One play later, Simms blasted over from 15 yards out as the Sooners built a 14-0 lead. The Sooners booted consecutive field goals following two stalled Ohio State drives for a shocking 20-0 lead.

Ohio State fought back and responded with 28 straight points in the second and third quarters. Ohio State got back on track with an 80-yard drive that culminated in a Springs 30-yard touchdown run. The Buckeyes then recovered a Lott fumble, which Gerald took in for another OSU touchdown on their next play from scrimmage. The extra point was good and the Sooners' lead had been cut down to 20-14.

Unfortunately, twice in the second quarter, Hayes decided to go for it on fourth down and failed, once at the 12-yard line, the other time at the 25-yard line. While he defended his actions after the game, not coming away with at least three points on either occasion would come back to haunt the Buckeyes.

Trailing 20-14 at the half, Ohio State's offensive explosion continued with its second drive of the third quarter. Buckeye freshman fullback Joel Payton wrapped up a 52-yard drive with a one-yard plunge for a touchdown. Ohio State had grabbed its first lead of the day, 21-20, following Vlade Janakievski's extra point attempt.

With the Buckeye fans going out of their minds, starting OSU defensive end Kelton Dansler picked off backup Sooners quarterback Dean Blevins's pass at Oklahoma's 33-yard line. Three plays later, Gerald suffered a head bump and was taken out of the game, replaced by Greg Castignola at quarterback. With 4:44 left in the third quarter, Castignola responded by firing a 16-yard touchdown pass to Jimmy Moore. Janakievski nailed the extra point and the Buckeyes' unlikely comeback looked to be complete. The lead swelled to 28-20.

With 6:24 left in the fourth quarter, Oklahoma recovered a Castignola fumble at the Sooners' 43-yard line. At that point, the roller coaster hit another big curve as the

Sooners marched 57 yards on 13 plays aided by an OSU offsides on a fourth-and-four situation at the 12-yard line. Peacock scored from one yard out just four plays later, as Oklahoma had pulled to within two points of the Buckeyes. With only 1:29 left to play in the game, the Sooners went for the all-important game-tying two-point conversion, but Peacock was stopped at the two-yard line.

Oklahoma kicker Uwe von Schamann laid down a perfect onside kick, which the Sooners recovered at the 50-yard line. With 1:21 left in the game, the Sooners moved the ball 27 yards in four plays down to the OSU 23-yard line. The key play was an 18-yard pass from Blevins to Steve Rhodes. Hayes then called a timeout in an effort to ice von Schamann with only three seconds remaining.

As the timeout wound down, the soccer-style kicker readied himself for the chance to be either a hero or a goat in the eyes of the Sooner nation. Following the timeout, von Schamann calmly lined up and booted his third field goal of the afternoon, a 41-yarder, to give Oklahoma a 29-28 victory over Ohio State. It was a stunning ending to one of the greatest games in Ohio State football history as the Buckeyes dropped to 2-1 on the young 1977 season. Afterward, a dejected Hayes told reporters, including the *Columbus Dispatch:* "We had our chances to win and we did not cash in on them. It was just like that. After they missed that attempt for a two-point conversion, I knew exactly what they were going to do. We practiced that onside kick every day. But we just messed it up and they turned their opportunity into the winning points."

In the second quarter, Ohio State twice decided to go for it on fourth down instead of kicking field goals, and both times failed. The first time was at the Oklahoma 12, the next on

the Sooners' 25. Hayes defended his decision not to go for three either time by saying: "We were behind in the game and we had to score touchdowns. No, I would do the same thing over again. I am the one who has to make the decisions; you are the people who can write about it."

While the Buckeyes sat dejectedly in their locker room, the Oklahoma locker room was deliriously happy with the last-second win. Switzer told the *Columbus Dispatch:* "I sure am glad that football games are only 60 minutes. This game had more drama, more tensions than any game I have been associated with. That last-second field goal had to be one of the greatest plays I have ever seen in intercollegiate football. Our team fought its guts out in a rugged game of 60 minutes of great football. It was like a miracle to get that last chance for the onside kick when things looked so dark for us."

Von Schamann, who had moved with his family from West Berlin, Germany, to Fort Worth, Texas, at the age of 14, kicked three field goals on the day, including the game winner with three seconds remaining. He told reporters in a raucous Oklahoma locker room: "There was no more pressure on that last one than on the other two. I knew I had to get off a good strong kick and I did. It was great!"

In the spring of 2004, Logan reflected back on the game by saying: "I was a senior co-captain and had been injured in the first game of the season against Miami with torn ligaments in an ankle. I sat out the game prior in the win over Minnesota and was questionable at best for the Oklahoma contest. When we got down 20-0 in the first quarter to the Sooners, Woody Hayes was absolutely beside himself. In our own place, getting embarrassed, and those of us on the sidelines, quite frankly, were wondering if it's going to be 50

to nothing. The speed of that football team was scary; it was unbelievable. But we also knew that they had a propensity of putting the ball on the turf. Pretty soon, they started fumbling the football and we started getting back into the game. The end of it was historic, obviously, with Uwe von Schamman kicking that field goal. The thing that I remember most about that game was after the field goal went through, my teammate and co-captain Aaron Brown, who had been playing nose guard, just lay flat on the field for what seemed to be an eternity. He could not move. He was totally spent, with emotions totally gone. I think that to this day, some 25 years later, people who were there still look at that football game and say that was the greatest game ever in Ohio Stadium. And to think that it was a loss is… almost disheartening."

On the following Monday, Oklahoma climbed to the top spot in the weekly AP poll while Ohio State fell to sixth.

SCORES BY QUARTERS	1ST	2ND	3RD	4TH	TOTAL
Oklahoma	17	3	0	9	29
Ohio State	0	14	14	0	28

1st Q-(OK) Peacock 23-yd TD (with fumble recovery) (7-0 OK)
1st Q-(OK) Sims 14-yd TD (14-0 OK)
1st Q-(OK) VonSchamann 23-yd FG (17-0 OK)
2nd Q-(OK) VonSchamann 33-yd FG (20-0 OK)
2nd Q-(OSU) Springs 30-yd TD (20-7 OK)
2nd Q-(OSU) Gerald 19-yd TD (20-14 OK)
3rd Q-(OSU) Payton 1-yd TD (21-20 OSU)
3rd Q-(OSU) Moore 16-yd TD from Castignola (28-20 OSU)
4th Q-(OK) Peacock 2-yd TD (Two point conversion failed—28-26 OSU)
4th Q-(OK) von Schamann 41-yd FG (29-28 OK)

1954

OHIO STATE 21, MICHIGAN 7

There were plenty of big games during Woody Hayes's 28 years as head coach of the Ohio State Buckeyes, but few were as important as the 1954 matchup with the Michigan Wolverines. Hayes had not been a popular choice to replace Wes Fesler as head coach of the Buckeyes in January of 1951. Many had hoped that Paul Brown, whose 1942 Buckeyes had won the national championship, would leave the Cleveland Browns and return for a second stint as head coach at Ohio State. Hayes's first three seasons were average at best. In 1951, Ohio State finished with a 4-3-2 record and a fifth-place finish in the Big Ten. The following season, the Buckeyes beat number one Wisconsin and later Michigan, but ended up with a third-place finish in the Big Ten and an overall record of 6-3. In 1953, OSU again posted a 6-3 record, but finished in fourth place in the conference. The Buckeyes finished the season by losing badly at Michigan 20-0, despite being a heavy favorite in the contest. Following the loss in Ann Arbor, many Ohio State fans began calling for Hayes's removal.

Years later, while addressing the *Columbus Dispatch* Quarterback Club during the 1975 season, Hayes related a story that would affect him the rest of his career. While sitting on his front porch during a summer evening in 1954, Hayes overheard a personal conversation between two neighbors concerning the Ohio State football program. One neighbor reportedly told the other: "This is the year we get Woody!"

Hayes said that comment provided him with additional inspiration to work as hard as he could every day: "I even got up an hour earlier each day, so I could prepare all the more for our season."

Not much was expected from the 1954 Buckeyes. The media selected OSU to finish no better than fifth place behind Illinois, Michigan State, Wisconsin and Iowa. It's hard to believe now, but Ohio State didn't open its season until September 25, a 28-0 home victory over Indiana. The Buckeyes then beat Pac-8 opponent California 21-12 before winning their first road game of the season, a 40-7 shocker at Illinois. The victory sent OSU to 3-0 on the season as they shot all the way up to fourth in the weekly Associated Press Poll.

Ohio State survived its closest call of the season on October 16th by winning at home over Iowa, 20-14. The Buckeyes' defense, which would play a key role later in the season against Michigan, held Iowa on downs inside their five-yard line with less than two minutes remaining in the victory. One of Ohio State's biggest tests of the season would come on October 23 as they broke open a close game with second-ranked Wisconsin.

OPPOSITE: OSU's Hubert Bobo (42) and company stop Michigan halfback Dave Hill on fourth and inches. (Ohio State University Photo Archive)

They won at home, 31-14. All-American Howard "Hopalong" Cassady's 88-yard interception return for a touchdown in the third quarter changed the momentum of the game as the Buckeyes improved to 5-0.

The Buckeyes then held off Northwestern by winning in Evanston 14-7 before a non-conference 26-0 victory at home over Pittsburgh. The OSU juggernaut was now in high gear as they played their final road game of the Big Ten season. Beating Purdue in West Lafayette, 28-6, moved them to 8-0 on the season and ready for a date with Michigan. For the first time since 1950, more than just pride was on the line for the winner of the Ohio State-Michigan contest. If Ohio State should win, they would be outright Big Ten champions. A victory by Michigan would mean that the two teams would share the conference championship and the Wolverines would go to the Rose Bowl by virtue of beating Ohio State in head-to-head competition.

When the Associated Press poll was released late on Monday, undefeated Ohio State had moved into the number-one spot by seven points over second-ranked and undefeated UCLA. Oklahoma was third, Notre Dame fourth with Michigan at 6-2, checking in at number 12.

Most former players will tell you that the games were easy compared to the practices, especially during Michigan week. The days leading up to the 1954 game were no different as running back Hop Cassady dislocated a finger while offensive lineman Jerry Williams bruised a knee. Quarterback Dave Leggett missed the first half of Tuesday's practice with a nasty rash, diagnosed as a reaction to a penicillin shot.

Temperatures for practice that week were unseasonably high. On Wednesday, Columbus recorded a high of 72 degrees, one short of the all-time high for November 17. Rain fell off and on during the day on Thursday, with a high of 70 degrees. Friday was another fantastic day, sunny skies and a high of 65 as of 1:30pm.

During the week, a *Collier's* magazine naming the publication's 65th All-Star football team arrived in Columbus. The starting offense, as named by Collier's, listed the following positions:

Ends: Max Boydston, Oklahoma; Don Holleder, Army.
Tackles: Jack Ellena, UCLA; Sid Fournet, LSU.
Guards: Jimmy Salsbury, UCLA; Bud Brooks, Arkansas.
Center: Kurt Burris, Oklahoma.
Quarterback: Ralph Guglielmi, Notre Dame.
Halfbacks: Dick Moegle Rice, Howard Cassady, Ohio State.
Fullback: Alan Ameche, Wisconsin.

Everything was on the line for Ohio State if they should beat Michigan: a perfect 9-0 season, an undisputed Big Ten championship, a trip to the Rose Bowl, and a possible national title. If Michigan could pull off the upset, the Wolverines would share the conference title and a vote by the Big Ten athletic directors would follow to determine the Rose Bowl representative for the conference.

As the days dwindled down to Saturday's game, the tension with Hayes became so thick you could cut it with a knife. Ever fearful of "spies" sneaking into practice, Hayes ordered sports writers along with a few privileged others attending practice on Thursday to wear practice jerseys so they could be readily identified. One of those having to wear the scarlet jersey included Dr. Walter Duffee, the OSU team physician for 35 years.

The annual "senior tackle" was held on Friday. Fifteen OSU seniors hit the sled one more time before heading to the golf course for their traditional dinner. Earlier in the day Leggett, who had been bothered by a severe rash earlier in the week due to a penicillin reaction, was admitted to University Hospital. Leggett recalled in March of 2004: "I had to go to the hospital because I was have difficulty breathing due to the reaction from the penicillin shot on Monday. I was in for eight hours as they pumped me full of medicine to combat the penicillin. Nobody knew if I was going to play the next day, it was so bad. But, the next day, I showed up and played."

A week's worth of great weather ran out on Saturday, November 20, 1954, as Ohio State hosted Michigan. A dreary, cold, wet afternoon greeted the 82,438 fans who showed up at Ohio Stadium. An estimated television audience of 80 million fans watched the *Game of the Week* as sportscasters Jack Drees and former Michigan All-American Tom Harmon, "Old 98," handled the call of the game with Bill Stern working the pregame and postgame commentaries.

After taking the opening kickoff, Michigan immediately went to its bag of tricks to confuse Ohio State. Using multiple formations and an unbalanced line (just one player, a guard, on the left side of the center), the Wolverines struck first by taking the opening kickoff and marching 68 yards for a touchdown. Halfback Dan Cline scored the touchdown from seven yards out on an exciting razzle-dazzle double handoff reverse. The extra point was good and the Wolverines led by a score of 7-0.

In the second quarter, Michigan drove the ball down to the OSU 14-yard line. Then Jimmy Rosenboro batted down two passes, including one in the end zone as the Wolverines settled for a field goal attempt.

Michigan end Ron Kramer, who doubled at times as a kicker, booted the short attempt wide left as the Buckeyes breathed a sigh of relief. With about 3:20 left in the second quarter, OSU second-string linebacker Jack Gibbs picked off Michigan quarterback Jim Madock's pass and raced 45 yards before being dragged down at the Wolverines' 10-yard line. Ohio State was assessed a five-yard penalty for delay of game following the big play by Gibbs, and the offense took over at Michigan's 15-yard line. On the next play, quarterback Dave Leggett tossed a touchdown pass to Fred Kriss. Tad Weed kicked the extra point and with 2:51 left in the second quarter, OSU had tied Michigan at 7-7.

Later, with a little over five minutes remaining in the third quarter, Ohio State sophomore Hubert Bobo came into the game and booted perhaps the worst punt in OSU history. With the ball on the Buckeyes' 21-yard line, Bobo punted the ball straight up into the air. Michigan downed the ball at the OSU 14-yard line. Four plays later, Michigan earned a first down at the OSU four-yard line. On first down, Wolverines halfback Dave Hill went straight up the middle for one. Next, Cline tried the same play, but was stopped for no gain. Hill then cut over his left guard for two yards, down to the one-foot line. Facing a fourth and less than a yard at the OSU goal line, the Buckeyes stuffed the Wolverines. The goal line stand remains to this day as one of the greatest defensive stops in OSU history.

With only 54 seconds left in the third quarter, Ohio State took over with the ball resting just shy of the one-yard line. In an effort to get away from their own goal line, Leggett called two straight quarterback sneaks that moved the ball out to the 10-yard line before time ran out and the teams switched ends of the field. On the second play of the fourth quarter, Cassady busted through the Michigan defense for 57 yards. Eight plays later, Leggett found Dick Brubaker on an eight-yard touchdown pass. Weed converted the extra point as Ohio State grabbed its first lead of the day by a score of 14-7.

Only seven minutes remained in the contest when Cassady picked off a Michigan pass at the OSU 26 and sped 13 yards before being brought down. Chewing up time and yardage, the Buckeyes put together a 12-play, 61-yard drive as Cassady plunged into the end zone from a yard out for the final touchdown of the afternoon. Weed kicked the extra point to give Ohio State a 14-point lead with only 44 seconds remaining as the Buckeyes went on to win by the score of 21-7.

Fans swarmed the field as they helped the Ohio State players carry Hayes off the field in celebration. For only the second time since 1944, Ohio State had beaten Michigan. In the process, the Buckeyes finished up their season at 9-0, while winning an outright Big Ten championship, a trip to the Rose Bowl and their second national championship in school history. They equaled a Big Ten record set by Chicago in 1913 by winning seven league games.

Afterward, in the locker room, the *Columbus Dispatch* reported that Hayes told his players: "Gentlemen, I have just one thing to say to you…" Then Hayes leaped high into the air and yelled, "Whoopee."

While the players celebrated by pouring cups of orange juice over one another, Hayes hugged Hop Cassady's father, Pearl, and said, "Did your boy play today?" Then in a more serious tone, he said, "If he [Hop] ever said it, I would boot him, but I'll say to you, that boy of yours is the the greatest football player I've ever seen."

On the day, Cassady carried the ball 14 times for 94 yards and a touchdown. Defensively, he intercepted a pass while helping out on the famous goal line stand. Fifty years later, Leggett recalled the turning point in the game by telling WBNS-AM in Columbus: "I remember big Jim Parker stopping up the middle and holding Michigan on the goal line. Then we took over on our half-yard line, ran a couple of quarterback sneaks and got a first down. Hop [Cassady] broke loose on a 57-yard run. Then we surprised them later on about the 10-yard line on a fake to Hop and a touchdown pass to Brubaker. Then Hop intercepted a pass and later scored right before the game ended. But Jack Gibbs got us going right before halftime with that big interception that set up our first score of the day. It was a great, great victory."

SCORES BY QUARTERS	1ST	2ND	3RD	4TH	TOTAL
Michigan	7	0	0	0	7
Ohio State	0	7	0	14	21

1st Q-(UM) Cline 7-yard TD (7-0 UM)
2nd Q-(OSU) Leggett to Kriss, 15-yd TD (7-7)
4th Q-(OSU) Leggett to Brubaker 8-yd TD (14-7 OSU)
4th Q-(OSU) Cassady 1-yd TD (21-7 OSU)

OPPOSITE: Don Schwartz (77), Dave Leggett (22), and the Buckeyes celebrate their win over Michigan. (Ohio State University Photo Archive)

1984

OHIO STATE 45, ILLINOIS 38

Both Ohio State and Illinois knew heading into the 1984 contest at Ohio Stadium that the loser would more than likely be out of the race for the Big Ten title. Only twice in the 88-year history of the conference had the champion had two league losses. The Buckeyes entered at 4-1 overall and 2-1 in the Big Ten. Illinois, the reigning outright Big Ten champions stood at 3-1 in the standings, 4-2 overall. In 1983, Illinois beat Ohio State for the first time in 15 seasons by a final of 17-13 in Champaign. The Illini went on to become the only conference team to go 9-0 in league play before losing in the Rose Bowl to UCLA. The Buckeyes felt it was payback time for what happened the previous season in Champaign.

On October 13, 1984, a homecoming crowd of 89,937 jammed into Ohio Stadium to watch the top two offenses in the Big Ten Conference lock horns. Most figured they'd probably be in for a pretty good game, but no one could have predicted what was in store for them as Illinois rocketed out to a quick 24-0 lead. First, Illinois put together an 11-play, 80-drive that culminated in a three-yard touchdown pass from quarterback Jack Trudeau to wide-open wide receiver Randy Grant. Illinois kicker Chris White, son of Illini head coach Mike White, booted the extra point as OSU trailed, 7-0. Illinois followed up with a 26-yard field goal by Chris White, as the lead was increased to 10-0.

Following the ensuing kickoff, Illinois defensive back Mike Heaven intercepted OSU quarterback Mike Tomczak's pass at the Buckeyes 21-yard line. Four plays later, Trudeau hit receiver David Williams on a nine-yard touchdown pass and Illinois' lead had grown to 17-0.

On the next series for Ohio State, running back Keith Byars fumbled on first down as Illini safety Craig Swoope recovered the ball at OSU's 21-yard line. Six plays later, Illinois tight end Cap Boso caught an eight-yard touchdown pass. The extra point was good and Illinois' lead had grown to 24-0 just 13 seconds into the second quarter. To say that the OSU faithful were a little disturbed by what they were seeing in the first quarter and a half's worth of action is like saying that the Titanic had a small leak.

Ohio State finally got on the scoreboard with 4:43 left in the second quarter as Byars scored from 16 yards out capping a nine-play, 91-yard drive. The key play in the drive was a 36-yard pass from Tomczak to wide receiver Cris Carter. The extra point was good as OSU cut the Illini lead down to 24-7. Not only did Illinois give up a touchdown, one of its star defensive players, safety Craig Swoope, was ejected from the game following a flagrant dead-ball personal foul on the touchdown. With a 15-yard penalty assessed on the kickoff, OSU tried an onsides kick that was recovered by linebacker Joe Jenkins on the Illini 31-

ABOVE: Tight end Jud Groza (85) grabs receiver Cris Carter following Carter's touchdown catch. Left guard Jim Lachey (64) and Bob Maggs (71) celebrate. (Ohio State University Photo Archive)

yard line. Two plays later, Tomczak connected with Carter on a 30-yard touchdown. Rich Spangler hit his second extra point of the day and Ohio State trailed Illinois, 24-14.

Illinois, desperate to stop the Ohio State momentum, went back to the air in an effort to set up its own score. Trudeau threw his first interception of the day as OSU roverback Sonny Gordon made a beautiful diving catch at Illinois' 38-yard line, giving the Buckeyes one more chance before the half. Ten plays later, Byars scored his second touchdown from four yards out. Spangler connected on the extra point and Ohio State now trailed Illinois

24-21 with only 23 seconds before the end of the first half.

Whatever Ohio State head coach Earle Bruce said at halftime worked. On the second-half kickoff, OSU's Steve Hill laid a vicious hit on Illinois' Ray Wilson, causing a fumble. William White recovered the ball at the Illini 26. Byars then carried the ball four straight times, powering his way in for his third touchdown of the afternoon. Spangler nailed his fourth extra point and for the first time on the day the Buckeyes led Illinois, 28-24.

Instead of folding their tents and calling it an afternoon, Illinois came right back as White booted a 46-yard field goal. The Illini cut the gap down to 28-27. Then, one of the greatest plays in Ohio Stadium history took place. With the Buckeyes at their 33-yard line, Byars took a hand-off from Tomzack and raced 67 yards down the east sideline towards the closed end of the stadium for his fourth touchdown of the day. Byars showed the nation he was capable of not only busting tackles, but also outrunning five defenders, all with sprinters' speed for the score. If that were not exciting enough, he ran the final 40 yards after losing a shoe! The extra point by Spangler was good as Ohio State's lead grew to 35-27 with 8:57 left in the third quarter.

In 2001, before he was to be enshrined into the Buckeyes "Hall of Fame," Byars reflected on the play in which he lost his shoe by saying: "That shoe run stands out. I felt the shoe coming loose and the next thing I know I said, 'Well, I can't stop now, I've got a chance at a big play,' and I kicked the shoe off and ended up scoring a touchdown. The next thing I know, big Jim Lachey brought the shoe to me on the sideline and it was still fully strung up. For whatever reason, it just fell off."

The excitement level at the horseshoe was at an all-time high. Any thoughts of sneaking out early to resume tailgating in the parking lots would have to wait. After leading at one point, 24-0, Illinois had been outscored, 35-3. If they couldn't respond on their next drive, the game would probably be lost. Illinois did respond by driving 63-yards for a touchdown with Trudeau hitting Ray Wilson on a nine-yard scoring pass to cut the OSU lead down to, 35-33. Trudeau then rolled to the right, into the end zone for a two-point conversion as Illinois tied the score at 35 with 1:09 left in the third quarter.

Ohio State and Illinois both traded field goals in the fourth quarter. Spangler nailed a 47-yarder with 10:21 left in the final period to give OSU a, 38-35 lead. Illinois came right back before being buckled down at their goal line. Instead of going for it at the OSU one-yard line, Illinois kicked a 16-yard field goal to tie the score at 38 with 3:18 remaining.

By this time, the crowd was near hysterics. The two teams had combined to put up nearly 1,000 yards in offense while scoring 76 points. After all they had been through, Ohio State's offense decided that a tie, or quite possibly a loss, was not an option as they ran onto the field. With Byars fast approaching an Ohio State single-game rushing record, the OSU offensive line came alive one more time marching 80 yards in 11 plays for another touchdown. Byars scored again from three-yards out on a pitch sweep to the left for his fifth score of the day. With 36 seconds remaining, Spangler booted his fifth extra point as the Buckeyes took the lead and hung on for a 45-38 victory.

Afterwards, *Columbus Dispatch* writer Tim May asked Bruce about rallying 24 points down early in the second quarter. He responded by saying: "I didn't see any eyes of defeat on the sideline. I don't know of anything more exciting in this stadium than the 24-0 comeback by the 1984 Buckeyes. This is the greatest comeback I've ever been associated with."

Columbus Citizen-Journal reporter Rusty Miller, (now with the Associated Press) asked Bruce what the turning point in the game was. He responded by saying: "I guess when I look at it, the big turning points was the 15-yard penalty on the onside kick (after Swoope penalty) that we recovered and then went in and scored. They let us get back in the ballgame before the half."

The greatest come-from-behind victory in Ohio State history wouldn't have been possible if not for Byars record-setting afternoon. The junior tailback rushed for an Ohio State record 274 yards on 39 carries, breaking two-time Heisman Trophy winner Archie Griffin's mark of 246 yards. He also tied Pete Johnson's OSU record of five touchdowns in a game. Byars would eventually finish second to Boston College quarterback Doug Flutie in the 1984 Heisman balloting.

Former All-America offensive lineman Jim Lachey, who now does color commentary for the Ohio State Football Radio Network, reflected on the game by saying: "I remember being down after losing the week before at Purdue (28-23) and coming out and being down 24 points and thinking, 'Oh my goodness, are we going to be able to pull this thing back?' I think a lot of guys kind of rallied along the sideline saying, 'Hey, we're not gonna get 24 points in one play, so let's take this one play at a time.' When we got close to the end of the second quarter we knew it was going to be a ballgame and of course the second half was incredible. I think personally, I remember running the same play about eight times in a row (23, 26 Dave). Byars picked up tons of yards to get the rushing record that day and just knowing that you're down a lot and you come back was great. No one wants to get down like that, but you remember the come back and it's just one of those games that I'll never forget."

Besides rallying from 24 points to beat reigning conference champion Illinois, Ohio State had positioned themselves nicely for a chance to win the Big Ten title. Having already beaten preseason league favorite Iowa, the Buckeyes at 5-1 overall, 3-1 in the conference, only had to face Michigan State, Wisconsin, Indiana and Northwestern before hosting Michigan for a chance to go to the Rose Bowl. The Buckeyes would beat the Spartans, before losing to the Badgers on October 27. Ohio State recovered to throttle the Hoosiers and Wildcats, before squaring off at home against Michigan. Byars scored three touchdowns, two of those to break open a tight game in the fourth quarter, as Ohio State topped the Wolverines 21-6. Unfortunately, the Buckeyes lost another heartbreaker in the January 1, 1985 Rose Bowl to USC, 20-17. OSU would finish up the season with a familiar record under Bruce at 9-3.

The panel voted the exciting 1984 Ohio State 45-38 win over Illinois as the eighth most memorable game in the last 50 years of Ohio State football.

SCORES BY QUARTERS	1ST	2ND	3RD	4TH	TOTAL
Illinois	17	7	11	3	38
Ohio State	0	21	14	10	45

1st Q-(ILL) Trudeau to R. Grant 3-yd TD (7-0 ILL)
1st Q-(ILL) C. White 26-yd FG (10-0 ILL)
1st Q-(ILL) Trudeau to R. Williams 9-yd TD (17-0 ILL)
2nd Q-(ILL) Trudeau to Boso 8-yd TD (24-0 ILL)
2nd Q-(OSU) Byars 16-yd TD (24-7 ILL)
2nd Q-(OSU) Tomczak to Carter 30-yd TD (24-14 ILL)
2nd Q-(OSU) Byars 4-yd TD (24-21 ILL)
3rd Q-(OSU) Byars 1-yd TD (28-24 OSU)
3rd Q-(ILL) C. White 46-yd FG (28-27 OSU)
3rd Q-(OSU) Byars 67-yd TD (35-27 OSU)
3rd Q-(ILL) Trudeau to Wilson 9-yd TD (Trudeau runs for a two-point conversion 35-35)
4th Q-(OSU) Spangler 47-yd FG (38-35 OSU)
4th Q-(ILL) C. White 16-yd FG (38-38)
4th Q-(OSU) Byars 3-yd TD (45-38 OSU)

THIS PAGE: Keith Byars crossing the goal line following his 67-yard touchdown in the third quarter. (Note: Byars ran the final 40 yards minus his left shoe.) (Brockway Sports Photos)

2002

OHIO STATE 14, MICHIGAN 9

For the first time since the 1996 season, Ohio State headed into its final game of the regular season against Michigan undefeated and untied. The Buckeyes entered the contest ranked second in the country with a perfect 12-and-0 record. Michigan was ranked ninth (9-2, 6-1), out of the Big Ten title hunt with an earlier loss to Iowa, but looking to spoil OSU's season.

The week leading up to the annual contest was at a fever pitch. Scalpers were selling tickets in the hundreds and even thousands of dollars for a pair of seats. A win over Michigan would send Ohio State to the national championship game. The Buckeyes' likely opponent would be top-ranked Miami in the Fiesta Bowl. If the Buckeyes lost to the Wolverines, Ohio State would be headed to a lesser bowl. While fans were enthusiastic about the upcoming contest, many couldn't help but remember the times that Michigan had ruined perfect regular seasons by the Buckeyes in 1969, 1973, 1995 and 1996.

On November 23, a stadium-record crowd of 105,539 witnessed one of the truly great games in Ohio State history. The outcome wasn't decided until the final play. Michigan won the toss and deferred to Ohio State. A geared-up Wolverines defense forced the Buckeyes to go three and out. Andy Groom punted the ball to Michigan's 28-yard line, where the maize and blue took over. The Wolverines' offense methodically moved the ball down field, gaining three first

downs down to Ohio State's 18-yard line. The Buckeyes' defense stiffened and Michigan was forced to kick a 36-yard field goal.

Freshman tailback Maurice Clarett entered the game for the first time with just over eight minutes to go in the first quarter. Clarett's presence on the field fired up the record crowd. It was his first appearance since a shoulder injury had sidelined him for two of the last three games. On his first play, he took a screen pass nine yards, then followed that with a seven-yard run. With the team and the crowd feeding on the emotion of Clarett's play, the Buckeyes began to move downfield.

Later in the drive, Clarett would blast through with a 28-yard run. On his next carry, Clarett was sent to the sidelines, clutching his left arm in pain. Everyone felt that his day was done. On the 10th play of the drive, Clarett re-entered the contest and swept into the end zone from the right side for the score. Following the extra point, Ohio State went on top, 7-3.

Michigan would come back with a pair of field goals, including one with just 16 seconds before halftime to grab a 9-7 lead. The Wolverines ran 30 plays from scrimmage in the second quarter compared with just five for Ohio State. Michigan's last possession was a 19-play, 88-yard drive, which ate up an incredible eight minutes and 24 seconds.

Ohio State's defense held in the third and fourth quarters, forcing Michigan to punt on each of its first four possessions.

ABOVE: OSU freshman running back Maurice Clarett crosses the goal line in the first quarter for the Buckeyes' first score of the day. (Jeff Brehm)

Chris Gamble returned the Wolverines' fourth punt of the day to OSU's 33-yard line. A 10-yard interference penalty let OSU start off in much better shape, seven yards shy of midfield.

On first down at OSU's 43-yard line, fullback Brandon Schnittker grabbed a pass that appeared to be headed to receiver Michael Jenkins. He advanced it 15 yards to Michigan's 42-yard line. Three plays later, Ohio State faced a critical juncture of the game. Faced with a fourth and one on UM's 33, would the Buckeyes try to kick a 50-yard field goal or go for a first down late in the fourth quarter? Quarterback Craig Krenzel urged head coach Jim Tressel to go for the first down. Tressel said he never really considered trying for the field goal, telling WBNS-AM: "I think Craig Krenzel would have killed me if I didn't let him continue that drive. He is very competitive and would have gone haywire."

On fourth and one at UM's 33-yard line, Krenzel powered the ball for the first down, keeping the drive alive. The Buckeyes then ran the throwback pass to Clarett, good for a 26-yard pickup down to UM's six-yard line. Clarett gained three yards over the right side to make it second and goal at UM's three. With tight end Ben Hartsock in motion and Schnittker positioned as if the Buckeyes would run over the left tackle, Krenzel then ran to the right side and pitched the ball to trailing tailback Maurice Hall. He crashed over the goal line, giving OSU a 14-9 lead with 4:55 remaining in the fourth quarter.

With everything on the line, it was time for the Buckeyes' defense to work its magic as it had all season long and stop the Wolverines. Michigan took over on its own 20 with 4:51 remaining. Michigan drove down the field to OSU's 30. On first down, Darrion Scott, who had terrorized opposing teams all season long, forced quarterback John Navarre to fumble. Defensive end Will Smith recovered for OSU

at the Buckeyes' own 36-yard line with 2:02 remaining in the contest.

The crowd at Ohio Stadium began to take their heart medicine and say their prayers. If the Buckeyes could gain a first down, OSU would be able to run out the clock and play in the Fiesta Bowl for the national championship. If Michigan could stop OSU, they would have one final crack at beating the Buckeyes. The Wolverines used their final two timeouts after each of the Buckeyes' first two plays. Clarett was then stopped on third down, gaining only two yards in three carries. Following a punt by Groom, Michigan started its make-or-break drive at its own 20-yard line with 58 seconds to play.

Navarre, using the clock effectively, moved his team down to the OSU 24. He then threw a pass out of the end zone with one second remaining. With time for one final play, could the Buckeyes' defense hang on as they had all season long?

In almost slow motion, Navarre's slant pass was intercepted by junior OSU safety Will Allen at the three-yard line, setting off a wild celebration. Ohio State defeated the team up north by a final score of 14-9. A sea of Buckeye fans stormed the playing field to celebrate with the players. For the first time since 1981-82, Ohio State had beaten the Wolverines in consecutive years.

The Wolverines led in first downs, 26-13, total offense, 368 yards to 264, and ran 92 plays from scrimmage compared to the Buckeyes' 49. In the end, OSU made plays offensively when it counted, while the defense held inside its red zone, allowing only three field goals.

Afterward, Ohio State senior safety Michael Doss was asked what he said to the team, trailing at the half, 9-7. "I said for the next 30 minutes, let's just lay it all out and leave everything on the field. I think every player responded and stepped his game up

ABOVE: OSU tight end Ben Hartsock (88) celebrates the 14-9 victory with the fans. (Jeff Brehm)

another notch and we played as a unit. When we felt it was time to make a stop, we had to make it, and we did that in the second half."

For the fifth time in its last seven games, OSU held the opposition scoreless in the second half while forcing two fourth-quarter turnovers, including Will Allen's interception, which clinched the victory. Afterward, on the Ohio State Football Radio Network, Tressel said: "I'll tell you what, you can't be any prouder of a young bunch then you are of these kids here. These coaches, they kept fighting and the crowd kept fighting. They got stunned for a second, but then they bounced back up and what an electric day!"

Fiesta Bowl representatives were on hand in the OSU locker room to officially invite the Buckeyes to play in the national title game. Ohio State's opponent would eventually be defending national champion Miami, who only needed to defeat Syracuse and Virginia Tech the following two Saturdays to face the Buckeyes. This set up the Fiesta Bowl battle of the only two undefeated teams left in Division 1-A.

With the victory, OSU improved to 13-0 overall, 8-0 in the conference, giving the Buckeyes a share of the Big Ten championship along with Iowa, who was also 8-0 in conference play. Unfortunately, Iowa and Ohio State did not face each other in 2002. Fans of both schools could only wonder which team was better.

In only his second season, Tressel had matched the number of victories his predecessor, John Cooper (2-10-1), had against Michigan over 13 seasons. While most associate the number 13 with being unlucky, 13 turned out to be a lucky number for Ohio State in 2002 as the Buckeyes acclumulated 13 victories with 13 seniors along with a sensational freshman tailback in Clarett, who wore the number 13.

SCORES BY QUARTERS	1ST	2ND	3RD	4TH	TOTAL
Michigan	3	6	0	0	9
Ohio State	7	0	0	7	14

1st Q-(UM) Finley 36-yd FG (3-0 UM)
1st Q-(OSU) Clarett 2-yd TD (7-3 OSU)
2nd Q-(UM) Finley 35-yd FG (7-6 OSU)
2nd Q-(UM) Finley 22-yd FG (9-7 UM)
4th Q-(OSU) Hall 3-yd TD (14-9 OSU)

1968

Ohio State 50, Michigan 14

While there were expectations that Ohio State might have a pretty good football team coming into the 1968 season, no one could ever have predicted that head coach Woody Hayes would capture his third Associated Press national championship. Ohio State had gone 6-3 the year before, good for fourth place in the Big Ten Conference. Many of the OSU starters were sophomores. Three of the four starters in the defensive secondary, both offensive halfbacks, along with quarterback Rex Kern, were starting for the first time.

Heading into its annual showdown with Michigan, OSU was 8-0 and ranked second nationally while the Wolverines were fourth in the country. Both teams were 6-0 in the conference. For the first time since 1964, Ohio State and Michigan would battle it out for an undisputed Big Ten championship and a trip to Pasadena. This would be Woody's fourth winner-take-all season finale.

In 1954, OSU broke away late for a 21-7 victory. In 1955, the Buckeyes won, 17-0, in Ann Arbor. In 1964, Michigan won, 10-0, in Columbus. Twenty-four times in the last 48 years, OSU and UM had won or shared the Big Ten football championship. The 1968 contest would now be added to the list.

The build-up for the 1968 contest between Ohio State and Michigan was tremendous. The last several years of the rivalry had left a lot to be desired. The Buckeyes entered the 1965 battle at 6-2 while Michigan was 4-5. Ohio State won by a final of 9-7. In 1966, Michigan beat OSU 17-3 as the Wolverines finished at 5-5, while the Buckeyes ended a disappointing season at 4-5. Then in 1967, Ohio State topped Michigan, 24-14. With the win, the Buckeyes finished at 6-3 while the Wolverines posted their second straight losing season at 4-6.

The 1968 OSU offensive line featured three seniors in tackles Dave Foley and Rufus Mays and center John Mullbach, along with junior guards Alan Jack and Tom Backhus. The backfield featured sophomores Rex Kern at quarterback and halfbacks Larry Zelina, Leo Hayden and John Brockington. Juniors Ray Gillian and Dave Brungard added considerable depth and talent at halfback while junior fullback Jim Otis received the lion's share of the carries. Sophomore Jan White anchored the tight end position while his classmate Bruce Jankowski ran the routes at wide receiver.

Sophomore middle guard Jim Stillwagon anchored the defensive line, which included veterans Vic Stottlemeyer, Paul Schmidlin, Brad Nielsen, and Bill Urbanik along with Dave Whitfield, Mike Radtke and sophomore end Mark DeBevc. Senior linebacker Mark Stier and sophomore Doug Adams clogged up the middle of the field. Adams had stepped in

OPPOSITE: Quarterback Rex Kern runs the ball early in the season against Northwestern. (Ohio State University Photo Archive)

for senior co-captain Dirk Worden, who had been lost for the season with a knee injury in the win against Purdue. Three of the four defensive backs were sophomores, Jack Tatum, Tim Anderson and Mike Sensibaugh. Junior Ted Provost, who returned an interception for a touchdown earlier in the season against the Boilermakers, provided the veteran leadership.

A then-record crowd of 85,371 fans filled Ohio Stadium on November 23, 1968, to watch Ohio State and Michigan fight it out for the Big Ten title. One of those who showed up for "the game" included golfer Jack Nicklaus and family. The former OSU golfer was suffering from a foot injury that curtailed his playing time, allowing him to attend.

Michigan, led by quarterback Dennis Brown and halfback Ron Johnson, jumped out to a quick 7-0 lead as Johnson scored scored the first points of the day on a one-yard run. Ohio State came back late in the first quarter to tie things up at 7-7. Fullback Jim Otis pounding the ball in with a five-yard touchdown run.

Early in the second quarter, OSU grabbed a 14-7 lead after quarterback Rex Kern ran it in from five yards out for a touchdown. Michigan came right back following a fumble recovery at OSU's 28-yard line and tied things up at 14 with Johnson scoring his second touchdown of the afternoon on a one-yard plunge. The Buckeyes' defense knew it had to stop Johnson if OSU were to have a chance of winning that afternoon. On the prior Saturday, he had rumbled for 347 yards and five touchdowns in the victory over Wisconsin.

With the scored tied at 14 in the second quarter, Kern drove OSU 86 yards in 17 plays for the go-ahead score as Otis scored again, this time from two yards out. The Buckeyes went ahead right before the half, 21-14.

Following halftime, Ohio State managed the only points of the third quarter, mounting an 11-play 72-yard drive that culminated in sophomore halfback Larry Zelina's score from six yards out. Jim Roman missed the extra point and the Buckeyes' lead was 27-14. The big play in the drive was Zelina's 21-yard sweep down to Michigan's nine.

A 13-point lead coupled with OSU's aggressive defense was too much for Michigan to overcome. Earlier in the game, defensive back Jack Tatum had set the tone by hitting Brown on the fourth play of the contest, causing a fumble that OSU defensive end Mark Debevc recovered. Brown had to be helped off the field by trainers before returning shortly after. Tatum also picked off one of three interceptions tossed by Brown.

Despite holding a comfortable 13-point lead heading into the fourth quarter, none of the Buckeyes felt as if they had the game in hand. The Wolverines had explosiveness with Johnson at halfback and Brown at quarterback. The question was, would the OSU defense be able to hold UM's offense in check for the final 15 minutes?

Following a Michigan punt early in the fourth quarter, Ohio State took over at its own 47-yard line. OSU's drive stalled at the Michigan 22-yard line. Facing a fourth and four, Jim Roman booted a field goal, giving OSU a 30-14 lead. Roman's field goal seemed to open the floodgates for the Buckeyes.

Trailing by 16 points and having to score, Michigan's next series proved to be disastrous. Doug Adams picked off a deflected pass by Brown, returning it down to the Wolverines' 31-yard line. Six plays later, Kern sneaked it in the final three yards for the touchdown. Roman's extra point this time was good, and the Buckeyes' lead was now 37-14.

On their next possession, the Wolverines were stopped short on a fake punt, giving Ohio State the ball on its own 33. OSU halfback Ray Gillian followed with a 50-yard reverse, setting up a two-yard plunge by Otis as OSU built a 44-14 lead.

At this point, the winner was cut and dry. Roverback Art Burton then picked off Dennis Brown's third interception of the day. Two plays later, Otis banged it in for six more, making the score 50-14.

As time wound down, the fans stormed the field. Thousands raced across the playing field, ripping down both goal posts, while enveloping Coach Hayes and the players. As the crowd chanted, "We don't give a damn for the whole state of Michigan," a snowstorm of paper confetti showered the field. Many more stayed in the stands celebrating the victory over "the team up north." For the first time since 1961, Ohio State had captured the Big Ten championship. It would be OSU's first Rose Bowl trip since 1958.

Some 36 years later, Kern looked back on the crush of people running onto the field to celebrate. "It was a phenomenon that hadn't occurred in the previous six or seven years. Of course the previous year they were hanging Woody in effigy, singing as they left the stadium, 'Goodbye Woody, we hate to see you go.' Then, in 1968, he's the greatest coach in the world. I've still never figured that out, but that's the way our fans are."

Afterward, Coach Hayes faced a packed locker room. He told the *Columbus Dispatch,* along with other reporters, "This is the best victory we ever had! This is a good football team. We beat the number four team in the country so convincingly, I believe we deserve to be rated number one now. A great victory, wasn't it?"

It couldn't have been lost on the 250 reporters covering the game that fans chanted, "We're number one," down on the field following the mauling of Michigan. Hayes went on to say, "This was a little more decisive than our championship wins over Michigan in '54 and '61. Besides, the '61 win didn't take us anywhere. The turning point of the game was Zelina's 59-yard kickoff return in the second quarter that was called back on a clipping call, and we still drove down the field to score before halftime."

In 2004, Kern told WBNS-AM in Columbus: "I was fortunate enough to play with a couple of Michigan guys in the NFL, and contrary to popular belief, they're not bad guys; they just wore the wrong uniforms."

The 50-14 victory was the second time that a Hayes team had scored 50 points against a Wolverines squad coached by Elliott. The other time had been back in 1961, when OSU clobbered Michigan in Ann Arbor, 50-20. Asked if he thought Hayes had poured it on in the end, Elliott responded firmly by saying, "I didn't think that he poured it on. In a ballgame like that, he's playing to win. No, I don't think that he poured it on."

In fact, following the touchdown that made it 50-14, the Buckeyes went for two, leading many to believe that Coach Hayes was in fact trying to run up the score. According to former halfback Larry Zelina: "Everybody thought that Woody was piling on at the end. The truth is, he couldn't get the special teams out on the field in time, so the offense just kept it and went for two."

While the Ohio State offense had scored 50 points in the victory, many of those points had been set up by a vicious Buckeye defense. Michigan quarterback Dennis Brown had been picked off three times, setting up three OSU touchdowns. Johnson, who had set an NCAA rushing record the week prior with 347 yards and five touchdowns against Wisconsin, was held to 91 yards and two touchdowns by the scarlet and gray. According

"He hadn't been stopped all year until he met us."

—Defensive back Jack Tatum

to Tatum: "He hadn't been stopped all year until he met us."

Kern reflected, "To this day, I can't believe that we won by that wide of a margin. It was a back-and-forth game in the first half. At halftime, one of the things we did was to make an offensive line change where we went with an unbalanced line. We put our two All-American tackles side by side, Dave Foley and Rufus Mayes. That gave us, on one side of the line, our guard and two tackles. We really dominated the second half, and it wasn't until the last three minutes of the football game that I looked up to the scoreboard and thought, you gotta be kidding me! We're not pushing 50 points, are we? It was just one of those days where everything went our way."

On the afternoon, the Ohio State offense rushed for 421 yards, led by fullback Jim Otis's 143 yards and four touchdowns. In the win, Otis broke two team records held by Howard "Hopalong" Cassady. The junior fullback from Celina would end up with 16 touchdowns on the season, one more than Cassady's single-season record of 1955, and 96 points, six better than Cassady's record that was also set in 1955. A sentimental Hayes would tell the *Dispatch:* "I doubt that I would have put Otis in for the last touchdown if I had been aware the score would break a team record held by Howard Cassady."

After the game, the fans celebrated. Thousands marched into downtown carrying parts of the destroyed goal posts onto the State Capitol grounds. Then, without incident, the celebrating crowd marched back north on High Street with a police escort. According to

the *Columbus Dispatch:* "One of the several marches downtown was topped at midnight with an appearance by coach Woody Hayes, most of the OSU marching band and cheerleaders on the west side of the Statehouse." Hayes told the mass of students, still carrying a portion of a goal post, "Boy, I thought they'd never get that thing out of the ground."

Later that night, police rushed all available uniformed personnel into the campus area shortly before 1:00 a.m. Reports of broken windows, street fighting and cars being overturned took place as students, undoubtedly bold with too much liquor in their systems, began to challenge the law. This, however, could not overshadow what a glorious day it had been in Columbus and for the Buckeye nation.

Looking down to the floor, slightly shaking his head, Kern would finish speaking of the 1968 win over Michigan by saying: "To this day, I'd wished we would have saved 13 points or so for the following year."

SCORES BY QUARTER	1ST	2ND	3RD	4TH	TOTAL
Michigan	7	7	0	0	14
Ohio State	7	14	6	23	50

1st Q-(UM) Johnson 1-yd TD (7-0 UM)
1st Q-(OSU) Otis 5-yd TD (7-7)
2nd Q-(OSU) Kern 5-yd TD (14-7 OSU)
2nd Q-(UM) Johnson 1-yd TD (14-14)
2nd Q-(OSU) Otis 2-yd TD (21-14 OSU)
3rd Q-(OSU) Zellina 6-yd TD (Ex. Point failed, 27-14 OSU)
4th Q-(OSU) Roman 20-yd FG (30-14 OSU)
4th Q-(OSU) Kern 3-yd TD (37-14 OSU)
4th Q-(OSU) Otis 2-yd TD (44-14 OSU)
4th Q-(OSU) Otis 2-yd TD (Ex. Point failed, 50-14 OSU)

ABOVE: Head coach Woody Hayes makes his viewpoint known with quarterback Rex Kern.
(Ohio State University Photo Archive)

1997 ROSE BOWL

OHIO STATE 20, ASU 17

A team and a season can sometimes be defined in one game. A single loss can ruin an entire year. A victory against a rival or in a championship-type setting can put a team on a pedestal for years to come. In 1996, Ohio State looked to have all the pieces in place for a run at the national championship. In 1995, Ohio State won its first 11 games before losing 31-23 at Michigan followed by a 20-14 loss to Tennessee in the Florida Citrus Bowl. It was an incredibly disappointing end to what had looked to be a season to remember. Heading into the 1996 season, the Buckeyes were determined not to let what happened in 1995 happen again.

The 1996 season started much like the season before with the Buckeyes beating their opponents in overwhelming style. On September 7, Ohio State pounded undermanned Rice, 70-7. The Buckeyes rolled up 632 yards of offense while scoring on 10 of their first 11 possessions. Seven different players scored, including a couple of freshman receivers, David Boston and Michael Wiley. Following an off week, OSU crushed Pittsburgh 72-0 before winning in South Bend, Indiana, 29-16 over Notre Dame. The Buckeyes opened the month of October with home wins over Penn State and Wisconsin before road wins at Purdue and Iowa.

Ohio State returned home on November 2 and beat Minnesota 45-0, but in the process lost tailback Joe Montgomery to a knee injury—so severe that I could hear the popping of Montgomery's knee from the enclosed press box. The Buckeyes then won at Illinois (48-0) before wrapping up a trip to the Rose Bowl by beating Indiana on the road, 27-17. In a key play, freshman linebacker Andy Katzenmoyer stripped Hoosiers quarterback Jay Rodgers of the ball. It was scooped up by defensive end Matt Finkes and returned 45 yards for a touchdown. Josh Jackson kicked a 31-yard field goal before safety Damon Moore returned an interception 28 yards to seal the victory. It would be the Buckeyes' first trip to Pasadena since the 1984 season.

While the game against Michigan wouldn't decide a trip to the Rose Bowl, an undefeated season and revenge for ruining OSU's perfect season from 1995 was on the line. Unfortunately, the Wolverines won in Columbus, 13-9, to ruin another undefeated season. A significant play happened right after halftime as Michigan wide receiver Tai Streets took a Brian Griese slant pass 69 yards for a touchdown after All-America cornerback Shawn Springs slipped and fell to the turf.

It was a weird ending to the season. In one respect, everyone was extremely disappointed about losing a chance to win a national championship by losing at home to Michigan. On the other hand, Ohio State would be playing in Pasadena. It was the first time ever that an Ohio State team lost to Michigan, yet played in the Rose Bowl. The Buckeyes had tied the Wolverines (7-7) in 1949 and again in 1973 (10-10) and played out west on New Year's Day, but never following a loss to Michigan. Following the loss to the Wolverines, OSU fell

**ABOVE: OSU linebacker Andy Katzenmoyer (45) directs
his blockers as he returns a Jake Plummer interception.
(Brockway Sports Photos)**

to fourth in the weekly Associated Press poll while its upcoming opponent, Arizona State, was undefeated and ranked second.

The bulk of the practice sessions leading up to the Rose Bowl were held during the first couple of weeks in December in Columbus. Ohio State practiced 10 times over 16 days in the Woody Hayes Athletic Facility. Unlike previous Rose Bowl appearances under former head coaches Woody Hayes and Earle Bruce, John Cooper allowed his players time to go home to be with their families for Christmas before flying out later that same day. Those who lived out of state were allowed to meet the team in Los Angeles.

After arriving on the west coast, the Buckeyes stayed 50 miles south of Hollywood in Costa Mesa, California, while holding their practice sessions at Orange Coast College. Several players, including quarterbacks coach Walt Harris, were bitten by the flu bug a couple of days after arriving. Usually, a prized trip to the Rose Bowl meant a mixture of fun and work for the players as a reward for winning the Big Ten championship. This time, however, OSU officials made it more of a business trip by not allowing the team to experience a prized trip to Disneyland while cutting down on all "extracurricular activities." Head coach John Cooper told the *Dispatch:* "The premium is absolutely on winning. Are you kidding me? It's win, win, win, win."

Two-time Heisman Trophy winning running back Archie Griffin, then OSU's assistant director of athletics and four-time Rose Bowl participant: "A bowl game used to be a bonus for an outstanding season. Any more, bowl games are games to see where you're going to end up in the polls."

One of the big storylines heading into the Rose Bowl matchup with Arizona State centered on Cooper, the other being quarterback Joe Germaine. Cooper had coached Arizona State from 1985 through 1987, leading the Sun Devils to a Rose Bowl victory over Michigan in 1987.

Germaine had grown up the Phoenix suburb of Mesa, Arizona, and attended Arizona State football games as a kid. Unfortunately, the Sun Devils didn't offer Germaine a scholarship. He turned down a $50,000 signing bonus to pitch for the Colorado Rockies to pursue his dream of being a college quarterback. Despite playing football for a year and graduating in three semesters from Scottsdale (Arizona) Community College, Arizona State was still not interested in the local product. Germaine then signed to play for Ohio State where he starred on the scout team for a year before alternating with Stan Jackson at quarterback during the 1996 season.

Two high-powered offenses would be hooking up in the Rose Bowl. Arizona State led the Pac-10 in total yards (492.5), rushing (248.6) and scoring (42.8). Quarterback Jake "The Snake" Plummer, who finished third in the Heisman Trophy balloting, threw for 2,575 yards, 23 touchdowns and nine interceptions. Junior tailback Terry Battle, who took over as the starter midway through the season, rushed for a school-record 18 touchdowns.

Ohio State finished first in the Big Ten in total yards (451.1), rushing (236.9) and scoring (39.5), but could only score two touchdowns in its final two games. Tim May of the *Columbus Dispatch* asked receiver Dimitrious Stanley about the late-season drop-off in production: "People always ask us, 'Why wasn't the offense getting any better?' Because we were doing a lot of the same things later on in the season we were doing at the beginning, when later on in the season you've got to change up a little bit to keep people on their toes. We weren't doing that."

As powerful as the Sun Devils' offense was heading into the Rose Bowl matchup, it would be facing a stiff opposition in the Ohio

State defense. The Buckeyes ranked second nationally versus the score (10.4) and number one in the Big Ten in total defense (243.3 yards per game). A pair of All-Americans led Ohio State, defensive end Mike Vrabel and Big Ten Coaches' Defensive Player of the Year cornerback Shawn Springs. Freshman middle linebacker Andy Katzenmoyer, who anchored the heart of the defense, was a second-team All-American.

On January 1, 1997, 100,635 fans showed up at the Rose Bowl to watch Ohio State battle Arizona State. Jackson, who had started the first 10 games of the season for Ohio State, before being replaced in the loss to Michigan by backup Joe Germaine, started the day at quarterback for the Buckeyes. Late in the first quarter, Jackson found freshman receiver David Boston on a nine-yard touchdown pass as OSU scored the first points of the day. Kicker Josh Jackson booted the extra point as Ohio State grabbed a 7-0 lead.

Midway through the second quarter, Plummer connected with Ricky Boyer on a 25-yard touchdown pass that many felt Boyer had dropped. The extra point was good and the score was tied at seven, where it would stay until halftime.

The Sun Devils took their first lead of the day with 9:12 left in the third quarter as kicker Rob Nycy's 37-yard field goal gave ASU a 10-7 advantage. Germaine, who had entered the game in the second quarter, kept the job in the third quarter and hit Stanley on a beautiful 72-yard touchdown pass, the longest pass play in OSU bowl history. Jackson kicked the extra point as OSU went back in front, 14-10, with 8:23 left in the third quarter.

With 8:06 left to go in the game and the ball at the Ohio State three-yard line, Jackson returned to quarterback the Buckeyes. Running back Pepe Pearson ripped off a 62-yard run. Five plays later, the drive stalled. ASU's Brent Burnstein then blocked Jackson's

38-yard field goal attempt as the Sun Devils took over at their own 41-yard line.

Plummer then led what many believed at the time to be the game-winning drive. Plummer's 26-yard lob to Lenzie Jackson brought the Sun Devils down to OSU's eight-yard line. Facing a third and goal from the 11, the slippery Plummer eluded an OSU blitz led by Katzenmoyer. "The Big Kat" grabbed at Plummer's jersey, but couldn't pull him down as he outraced defensive tackle Winfield Garnett to the end zone and the touchdown. The extra point was good and Arizona State led 17-14 with only 1:40 left in the fourth quarter. Katzenmoyer would later tell the *Columbus Dispatch*: "I thought the game was over then. I was just praying to God upstairs that we could come down and still at least score a field goal."

Much to the chagrin of Jackson, Germaine was brought back into the game to lead the Buckeyes' attempt in the two-minute drill (actually 1:40). Fullback Matt Keller returned the ensuing kickoff 15 yards to the OSU 35-yard line. With a heavy mist beginning to shroud the stadium, and the Rose Bowl crowd on its feet, Germaine began to lead Ohio State back down the field. The quarterback, who wasn't good enough to earn a scholarship from the school he loved to watch as a child, connected with Stanley three times for 11, 13 and 12 yards (two of those on third down plays), to the ASU 29-yard line. Two blatant pass interference calls moved the ball to the Sun Devils' five-yard line with only 24 seconds remaining. Ohio State fans around the world could only hope and wonder whether the Buckeyes could pull it out for one of the greatest victories ever or have to endure another crushing defeat.

Germaine brought the team to the line of scrimmage, barked out the cadence and dropped back to pass. With everything seemingly in slow motion, Germaine checked off

ABOVE: The Buckeyes pose for a picture in the locker room with the Rose Bowl trophy. Back L-R: linebackers Jerry Rudzinski and Ryan Miller (43) along with defensive coordinator Fred Pagac. Front L-R: fullback Matt Keller (23) and linebacker Greg Bellasari (30). (Courtesy of Ryan Miller)

his primary receiver in Stanley, who had drawn double-coverage and instead flipped a short toss to Boston, who back-pedaled into the end zone for one of the biggest touchdowns in Ohio State history. Jose Jackson attempted the all-important extra point, which was blocked by Burnstein, the same ASU player who had blocked his earlier field goal. Instead of having a four-point lead, the Buckeyes led by only three points at 20-17 with 19 seconds remaining on the clock. Fortunately for the Buckeyes, Plummer's magic ran out, as did the time. Ohio State hung on for its first Rose Bowl victory since 1974, beating ASU 20-17.

Pandemonium broke out on the field as the clock expired and thousands of Ohio State fans rushed the field. The hero of the game, quarterback Joe Germaine, was awarded the game's MVP while head coach John Cooper was nearly moved to tears, exclaiming, "It's the greatest moment in my 35 years of coaching!" Afterward, *Columbus Dispatch* columnist Bob Hunter asked Cooper, "Has a personal burden finally been lifted from your shoulders?" Cooper couldn't help but smile before he answered, "Until we play another game."

SCORES BY QUARTERS	1ST	2ND	3RD	4TH	TOTAL
Ohio State	7	0	7	6	20
Arizona State	0	7	3	7	17

1st Q–(OSU) Jackson to Boston 8-yd TD (7-0 OSU)
2nd Q–(ASU) Plummer to Boyer 25-yd TD (7-7)
3rd Q–(ASU) Nycz 37-yd FG (10-7 ASU)
3rd Q–(OSU) Germaine to Stanley 72-yd TD (14-10 OSU)
4th Q–(ASU) Plummer 11-yd TD (17-14 ASU)
4th Q–(OSU) Germaine to Boston 19-yd TD (Ex. Point failed— 20-17 OSU)

**ABOVE: Ohio State receiver David Boston (9) celebrates his
game-winning touchdown reception. (Brockway Sports Photos)**

1969

Michigan 24, Ohio State 12

November 22, 1969, is a day that will live in the memories of all Ohio State football fans. The Buckeyes, heavily favored for the contest in Ann Arbor, had been labeled that season as one of, if not the, finest teams in college football history. All Ohio State needed to reach that distinction was a victory over the Wolverines. Instead, it went down in one of the school's greatest defeats.

Heading into the 1969 battle at Michigan, the reigning national champion Buckeyes had steamrolled through their season, going 8-0. Ohio State had beaten its previous eight opponents by an average score of nearly 46-9. The OSU offense had scored over 40 points in every game but two, and in two games they had 62 points. The Buckeyes' defense had shut out two opponents while allowing three other teams a total of 20 points.

The "Super Sophomores" were now juniors and defending their Big Ten championship along with their national championship. No one really expected the Wolverines, 17-point underdogs, to derail the Buckeye Express, except first-year head coach Glenn "Bo" Schembechler.

Schembechler, a former assistant at Ohio State from 1958-1962 under Woody Hayes, had taken over for Bump Elliott in December of 1968. Following the 50-14 shellacking at Ohio State in 1968, Elliott had been re-assigned at Michigan as an assistant director of athletics under new athletic director Don Canham. A native of Barberton, Ohio,

Schembechler had been the head coach at Miami the previous six years, running up an impressive 40-17-3 mark in Oxford. Those in college football knew Schembechler was ready for the move.

On that cold November 22, 1969, afternoon in Ann Arbor, 103,588 fans, a national record for a regular-season football game, jammed inside Michigan Stadium for the start of what would be known as "The 10-Year War." The teacher, Woody Hayes, against his disciple, Schembechler. OSU was rated number one in the country at 8-0 while 12th-ranked Michigan had won its last four games to improve to 7-2 overall. Others had warned Schembechler the week heading into the contest that his team was going to get too high. His response: "Nah, let 'em get higher, because I don't think that you can get too high. The reason is that these teams have been in big games before. Both teams will be pretty highly emotional."

It looked early on that the Buckeyes would have their way with the Wolverines. In their second possession of the game, halfback Larry Zelina set up the first score of the day by returning a punt down to Michigan's 16-yard line. Later, senior fullback Jim Otis scored from one yard out to give Ohio State a 6-0 lead with 7:38 remaining in the first quarter. Stan White's extra point attempt failed and the Buckeyes' lead stayed at 6-0.

Michigan came right back, driving 55 yards in 10 plays as Garvie Craw scored from

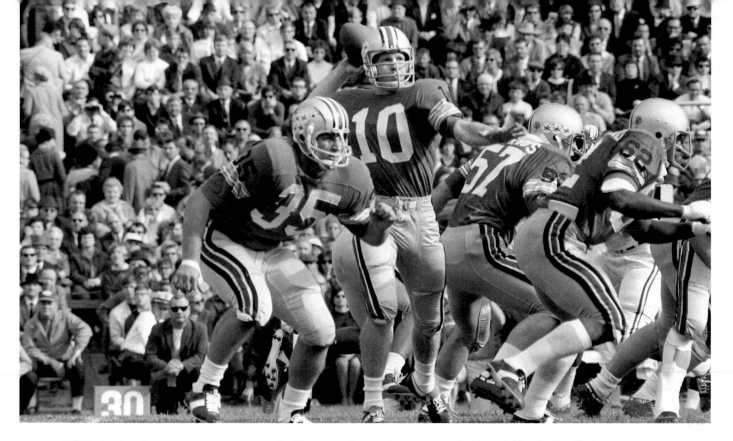

ABOVE: QB Rex Kern (10) fires a pass as Jim Otis (35), Tom Backhus (57) and Phil Strickland (62) block up front. (Brockway Sports Photos)

three yards out. The extra point attempt was good, and for the first time since the Rose Bowl, OSU trailed in a contest, 7-6, late in the first quarter.

The Buckeyes knew they were in for a fight early and bounced right back with a 10-play, 73-yard drive. Quarterback Rex Kern found end Jan White twice on the drive, once for 27 yards down to the Michigan 30. Then, on the first play of the second quarter, Kern hit White on a third and 14 at the Michigan 22, with White taking the ball over the middle for a touchdown. This time White made the extra point and Ohio State led, 13-7. Michigan was flagged for offsides, and Hayes elected to take the point off the board and go for a two-point conversion.

For Kern, remembering back to when Hayes decided to take the point off the board and go for two was painful: "I think that the critical play for us in that game was the extra point. Woody took the point off the board, and instead of being up 13-7, we're only up

12-7, trying to make it 14-7. We decided to run a quarterback sweep and we're a yard and a half away from the end zone. With both guards pulling, Michigan defensive end Cecil Prior broke through and tackles me to keep the score at 12-7. That's where the momentum changed at that point in time and all of a sudden, you could see Michigan get better and better."

The Wolverines fought right back to take the lead for good, as Craw scored from five yards out, capping a 67-yard drive. The extra point was good and Michigan now led, 14-12. The big plays in the drive included a 19-yard pass by quarterback Don Moorehead and a beautiful open-field 28-yard run by sophomore tailback Billy Taylor. Like an avalanche heading down a mountain, Ohio State was beginning to feel the full brunt of a fired-up Michigan squad.

Later in the second quarter, Barry Pierson returned a Mike Sensibaugh punt 60 yards to the OSU three-yard line. Two plays later,

Moorehead ran the ball in from three yards out for another Wolverines touchdown. The extra point was good and Michigan led, 21-12, with 10:10 remaining.

The Buckeyes then moved the ball down to the Wolverines' 27, but an 11-yard loss by Kern on a pass play ended the drive. Stan White's 53-yard field goal try fell short.

Somebody had forgotten to tell the Wolverines' offense they were not supposed to be able to move the ball on the vaunted Ohio State defense. On the very next series, Michigan marched it down the field again. A penalty nullified a great catch in the end zone by Jim Mandich as the Wolverines settled for a 25-yard field goal by Tim Killian with 1:15 left in the first half.

That's the way the first half ended in Ann Arbor, as the number one Buckeyes ran off the field, stunned, trailing Michigan, 24-12.

It could have been worse. Michigan defensive back Tom Curtis intercepted a Kern pass, setting up the Wolverines at OSU's 32-yard line. On first down, the Buckeyes' Ted Provost managed to tip a pass away in the end zone that Sensibaugh picked off to end the threat.

In the second half, Ohio State mounted a few drives, only to fall short. Michigan picked off six passes on the afternoon, three by Pierson. The Buckeyes defense held Michigan to four field goal attempts, all missed by Killian. As the clock wound down to end the game, fans poured onto the field. Just as the Ohio State fans had celebrated the year prior in Columbus, this time it was Michigan fans celebrating and tearing down the goal posts.

Many had said heading into the game that Ohio State had the greatest collegiate team ever assembled. The loss ended the Buckeyes' 22-game winning streak, their 17-game Big Ten winning streak and a shot of repeating as national champions. The Buckeyes suffered what some historians say is not only the great-est upset in Ohio State history, but Big Ten history as well.

Thirty-five years later, clasping his hands, hunched over with a grin on his face, a now slightly graying but distinguished Kern could only chuckle and say, "Well, it's interesting, ah, really interesting, devastating. What happened really was, I think that Bo was in our huddle, I really do. It was amazing. I had a bad day throwing the football [four interceptions], we had too many mistakes, and again, it felt as if Bo was in our huddle offensively because he knew exactly what we were going to be doing. He just knew Woody so well after working for him all those years."

The offensive stats were virtually the same for both teams. Ohio State outgained Michigan 377-374, but it was the six interceptions thrown by Ohio State that turned the tide for the Wolverines. Somewhat forgotten in the loss was the fact that Otis set a new Ohio State career rushing record that afternoon. Otis gained 144 yards to lift his career total to 2,524. The previous high had been 2,466 by Howard "Hopalong" Cassady, who played from 1952-55. According to Otis, "Records don't mean much if you lose."

Zelina would reflect some 35 years later on the Buckeyes. "We spoiled Woody a little bit when we were there; he spoiled us, but we spoiled him. There was never a situation where he asked us to do something that we didn't pull off. Regardless of how conservative we got offensively, we had so many great ath-letes that we were able to pull it off where the average team might not have done. When we got to that '69 Michigan game, we had six turnovers. I question if we had six turnovers in the previous five games. But we went to doing things that we hadn't done all year in a tight ballgame, and it cost us."

For Schembechler, the win locked up a trip to the Rose Bowl, the first for the Wolverines since the 1964 season. Bo would say in later years: "Woody told me I would never have a greater victory, and he was right. It was Woody's greatest team; he admitted that. It was my first year; I was trying to establish myself. Woody was surprised when I was named head coach, and whether people realized it or not, it was going to add a little something to the rivalry. I was brought to Michigan for one reason and one reason only: to beat Ohio State. He just didn't anticipate that someone who knew so much about him and his football would suddenly be on the other side, especially at Michigan."

Having the opportunity to coach against his old mentor was too much for Schembechler to pass up.

While Woody refused to allow the press in the locker room after the game, Schembechler was more than happy to talk. According to the *Columbus Dispatch*, Schembechler said, "I did say early this week that I felt we could beat Ohio State. You guys thought I was crazy, but I believed it. We wanted to run, avoid mistakes and stay close to them. Other teams get beaten by Ohio State by making mistakes early and getting behind. Then they can't catch up. We felt that if we were close at halftime, we would have a chance to win it."

Even an hour after the game, Schembechler continued to shake his head saying: "It's hard to believe…seems impossible…who would have believed it? I'll be honest with you; these are the same type kids we had at Ohio State. They're good kids, they really are. That's why we were able to become a good football team."

Following a 20-minute cooling-down period, Coach Hayes shooed away the reporters gathered outside the Ohio State locker room and told them: "Like every good thing, it had to come to an end. The second half, our offense didn't play well. The second half, our offense was miserable. We made every mistake possible. How many interceptions did we have? Six and a fumble near the end. That tells the story." Hayes then shoved his way back into the locker room, saying twice, "We just got beat, that's all." With that, he closed the door.

After a long bus trip home, Hayes went directly to his office to begin preparations for next year's home contest against Michigan. That spring, Hayes had a rug made that the players walked over as they headed out to practice. It read:

1969
MICH 24
OSU 12

1970
MICH
OSU

Ohio State would finish fourth in the Associated Press poll that season with an 8-1 record. The 1968 season saved Woody's job as Ohio State's dominance in college football had been reignited. The 10-year war between Bo and Woody was now underway.

SCORES BY QUARTER	1ST	2ND	3RD	4TH	TOTAL
Ohio State	6	6	0	0	12
Michigan	7	17	0	0	24

1st Q-(OSU) Otis 1-yd TD (Ex. Point missed- 6-0 OSU)
1st Q-(UM) Craw 3-yd TD (7-6 UM)
2nd Q-(OSU)Kern to White 22-yd TD pass (Extra point was good, but UM penalized for offside. OSU then opted for a two-point conversion which failed (12-7 OSU)
2nd Q-(UM) Craw 1-yd TD (14-12 UM)
2nd Q-(UM) Moorehead 2-yd TD (21-12 UM)
2nd Q-(UM) Killian 32-yd FG (24-12 UM)

1968

Ohio State 13, Purdue 0

For many years, most experts considered Ohio State's 13-0 beating of number one-ranked Purdue as the finest in OSU football history. While it is no longer considered the greatest game of all time, the importance of this victory cannot be overstated.

In 1967, Purdue had crushed Ohio State, 41-6. The 35-point loss to the Boilermakers was the largest margin of defeat during head coach Woody Hayes's 276 games at Ohio State. It was the Buckeyes' second loss in just the season's third game and their seventh defeat in the last eleven games over two seasons. Fan criticism of Hayes was more intense than ever. Following the loss to Purdue in 1967, OSU barely squeaked past Northwestern before losing to Illinois in front of a stunned homecoming crowd at Ohio Stadium.

The following week, Hayes told his assistant coaches that if they didn't win their remaining four games, they would probably be let go after the season. The Buckeyes proceeded to beat Michigan State, Wisconsin, Iowa and Michigan to finish up their season at 6-3. The saving grace was probably the victory in Ann Arbor, which gave Hayes an 11-6 overall record against the Wolverines.

Anticipation heading into the 1968 season was high. OSU had recruited well throughout the country during recent years. The football program finally overcame the OSU Faculty Council's "no-vote" in 1961, which prevented them from attending the 1962 Rose Bowl. Defensive backs Jack Tatum and Tim Anderson, tight end Jan White, split end Bruce Jankowski along with halfback John Brockington were sophomores from out of state who were all starting. Some of the state's best talent was also returning to the ranks as well. Quarterback Rex Kern out of Lancaster, Ohio, wingback Larry Zelina from Cleveland and linebacker Mark Debevic out of Geneva, Ohio, were just a few of the talented high school players who decided to attend Ohio State in 1967.

The Buckeyes opened the season with a 35-14 win over Hayden Fry's Southern Methodist University squad. Sophomore quarterback Rex Kern made a play during the game that only champions seem to make. On a fourth and 10 at the SMU 41, Kern quickly broke the team from the huddle while Coach Hayes was trying to send in the punt team. Kern made 15 yards on an option around right end to keep the drive alive. Years later, Kern told WBNS-AM in Columbus: "If I hadn't made the first down, Woody for sure would have put me on the bench, maybe for the rest of my career." OSU would beat Oregon, 21-6, and set up a "revenge" game against Purdue.

Heading into the Big Ten opener for Ohio State, Purdue was ranked number one in

OPPOSITE: OSU defensive back Ted Provost (46) brings down Purdue running back Leroy Keys. (Brockway Sports Photos)

the AP poll, OSU fourth. The Boilermakers, at 3-0, were a solid 13-point favorite in the contest and the preseason pick to win a second consecutive league title. Ohio State didn't just practice for Purdue in the week leading up to the game; the seeds were sown following the 41-6 loss to the Boilermakers in 1967, setting off a year's worth of preparation. According to former OSU safety Jack Tatum: "Coach Hayes had us remember two numbers, 15 and 32: the numbers worn by quarterback Mike Phipps and running back Leroy Keys. They were the two guys who had killed us the year before."

Keys, the 6'3", 205-pound senior running back was the team's leading rusher and was also a leading candidate for the 1968 Heisman Trophy Award. Phipps, who finished third among college quarterbacks in passing with 2,020 yards in 1967, had passed for 521 yards in Purdue's first three games of 1968. Besides Purdue's offensive juggernaut, its defensive line was huge, averaging nearly 6'5" and 258 pounds.

October 12, 1968, turned out to be a gorgeous afternoon, and a record crowd of 84,834, was on hand to witness the showdown at the Shoe. Purdue's offense had averaged 41 points per game in its first three contests of the season. The hope was that OSU's young defense could keep it close and create a few turnovers for the offense to capitalize on in the contest.

Three times in the first half, Ohio State's offense drove deep into Purdue territory, but all three times came away without any points. One drive was stopped at the four-yard line and all three times the Buckeyes failed on their field goal attempts.

Defensively, Ohio State limited the running and pass catching of Purdue halfback Leroy Keys while quarterback Mike Phipps was constantly under the gun from the Buckeyes' fierce rush and fine coverage. The

OSU offense lost halfback John Brockington to a sprained ankle, and Buckeyes linebacker and co-captain Dirk Worden's season ended with a severe knee injury. Neither team could put up any points in the first half, and the score remained tied at 0-0. The fact that the young OSU defense was able to keep the top-ranked Boilermakers off the scoreboard was a victory in itself.

On the third play of the third quarter, Tatum nearly intercepted an outcut pass by Phipps. The next play proved fatal for Purdue as Phipps, under heavy pressure, tossed an interception to defensive back Ted Provost, who returned it for 35 yards and a touchdown, giving OSU a 6-0 lead. Credit Ohio State secondary coach Lou Holtz for helping set up the pick. Following Tatum's near interception on the previous play, Tatum and Provost had switched off, with Tatum covering deep and Provost watching the flat. When Phipps saw Tatum go deep, he threw an outcut pass for a second straight play. With Provost waiting, he picked off the ball and returned it for the Buckeyes' first points of the afternoon. Jim Roman missed the extra point attempt as the Buckeyes clung to a precarious 6-0 advantage over the powerful Boilermakers.

Late in the third quarter, with Ohio State still leading by a score of 6-0, sophomore middle guard Jim Stillwagon intercepted another Phipps pass and returned it to the Boilermakers' 25-yard line. Four plays later, Kern was shaken up by a late hit out of bounds and replaced by senior quarterback Bill Long.

For Long, it was the moment he had been waiting for. A starter the previous two seasons, he watched from the sidelines the first two and a half games of the 1968 campaign after Kern beat him out for the starting quarterback position during the fall camp. On his

ABOVE: Rex Kern looks to pass as fullback Jim Otis (35) blocks Purdue's Billy McKay (88). (Brockway Sports Photos)

first play from scrimmage, Long found his main receiver covered as he dropped back to pass, tucked the ball and raced up the middle 14 yards for a touchdown, giving OSU a 12-0 lead. This time, Jim Roman's extra point attempt was good as the Buckeyes led 13-0.

Early in the fourth quarter, Tatum hit Phipps so hard that it may have affected him not only for the rest of the season, but during his NFL career as well. According to Zelina: "Mike Phipps was never the same after that Ohio State-Purdue game. He never was the same. I was a rookie in 1971 with the Cleveland Browns while it was Phipps's second year after being their first-round pick in '70. Our defense had hit him so hard in '68 that he was never the same quality quarter-

back. Phipps's performance for the rest of the '68 season never compared to his 1967 season."

Between Ohio State's running attack and a superb defensive effort, Purdue could not manage any points on the afternoon. The Buckeyes atoned for their 41-6 loss the year prior to the Boilermakers by beating number-one Purdue, 13-0.

The 1968 victory over Purdue was the coming-out party for Tatum and the rest of his teammates. During a 2004 interview on WBNS-AM, Tatum said: "It was one of those games where everyone came out and was ready to play. We thought maybe, if we could hang in there and keep it close, we'd be all right. Even though the halftime score was

"Even though the halftime score was tied, we felt that we were winning the game already because we felt that we had outplayed them. We felt that we could come out and beat them in the second half, and we did."

—Safety Jack Tatum

tied, we felt that we were winning the game already because we felt that we had outplayed them. We felt that we could come out and beat them in the second half, and we did."

Afterwards, with his shirt tail hanging out, his tie outside his collar, hugging a football and sipping a cup of water, Coach Hayes told the media, including the *Columbus Dispatch:* "Let me say this without equivocation, that was the greatest defensive effort I have ever, ever seen. It was unbelievable. That team was averaging 40 points per game and our kids shut them out and took them apart, with a splendid sustained effort."

Dick Otte of the *Dispatch* wrote that someone had informed Coach Hayes after the game that Purdue's assistants in the press box had told Jack Mollenkopf during the game that OSU had taken away Keys's running game. Hayes responded by saying: "If that's true, that's the finest compliment that I've ever had."

Although the Ohio State offense marched up and down the field all afternoon, the only points they could manage were backup quarterback Billy Long's 14-yard touchdown run. Offensively, the Buckeyes outgained Purdue 411 to 186 total yards. OSU had 22 first downs to the Boilermakers' 16. Ohio State rushed for 354 yards on the afternoon with junior fullback Jim Otis carrying the ball 29 times for 144 yards.

According to Kern: "We tried to run as many offensive plays as we could that day. Coach Hayes had taken a page out of Upper Arlington High School football coach Marv Morehead's playbook, where they ran a no-

huddle offense. The reason was it was going to be a warm day in Ohio Stadium and we were trying to run as many plays as we could in an effort to wear them down. Offensively, we just didn't score a lot of points. We ran a lot of no-huddle that season."

The Buckeyes' defense was able to hold the Boilermakers' offense, which had been averaging 41 points in winning their first three starts, scoreless for the first time in 24 games. The swarming Buckeyes sacked Phipps four times while returning one of two picks for a touchdown. The other interception set up Ohio State's only offensive touchdown of the afternoon. Purdue running back Leroy Keys was held to just 19 yards rushing on only seven carries.

Afterwards, a somewhat dazed Purdue head coach Jack Mollenkopf admitted to the *Columbus Dispatch:* "We just got clobbered."

While each generation has its own favorite or most important Ohio State football game in its memory banks, the 1968 win over top-ranked Purdue set the table for a national championship that season along with six shared or outright Big Ten titles during an eight-year stretch. If they had lost to the Boilermakers, who knows what the Buckeyes would have accomplished.

SCORES BY QUARTER	1ST	2ND	3RD	4TH	TOTAL
Purdue	0	0	0	0	0
Ohio State	0	0	13	0	13

3rd Q-(OSU) Provost 35-yd interception return for TD (Ex. Point failed, 6-0 OSU)
3rd Q-(OSU) Long 14-yd TD (13-0 OSU)

1969 ROSE BOWL

Ohio State 27, USC 16

Before the 2003 national championship game between number-one Miami and second-ranked Ohio State, the Buckeyes played in another national title game back on New Year's Day of 1969. Ohio State's 1968 season had produced a record of 9-0 and the nation's number-one ranking, while USC was ranked second at 9-0-1. For the first time in the 23 meetings between the Big Ten and the Pac-8 at the Rose Bowl, number one would face number two in the bowl game. The magnitude of the contest was nowhere near what it would be today, but it was still enormous. The Buckeyes had won the Big Ten championship with 13 starting sophomores. The Trojans, who had won the 1968 Rose Bowl 14-3 over Indiana, returned Heisman Trophy-winning tailback O.J. Simpson.

The Associated Press decided to take a final poll following the New Year's Day games. The AP made the change after the 1965 season, when its first six teams played in bowl games. Alabama, which had been ranked fourth, won the 1965 championship by knocking off third-ranked Nebraska. Meanwhile, top-ranked Michigan State and second-ranked Arkansas suffered their first defeats of the season.

After beating Michigan back in November, the Buckeyes jumped to the top ranking in the AP poll. The UPI trophy, as voted on by the coaches, already belonged to Ohio State, as did the "Mac Arthur Bowl," which was voted on by the National Football Foundation and Hall of Fame. The AP and the football writers had waited the last several years to present their award after the bowl games. *The Columbus Dispatch* quoted Ohio State head coach Woody Hayes as saying: "We won the national championship a month ago, on the regular season. We don't have to win it again. That's double jeopardy."

According to OSU senior linebacker Mark Stier: "There's a lot more at stake than just the Rose Bowl. USC coach John McKay said we shouldn't be No. 1 because we only played nine games and didn't play Notre Dame. We've got to prove we're No. 1. It's college football's super bowl."

Hayes worked the team hard the two weeks prior to the Rose Bowl, practicing virtually nonstop in California. A trip to Disneyland and Knotts Berry Farm, along with several dinners, relieved the players' strain from the heavy practices.

Unlike the Buckeyes' last visit to the Rose Bowl back in 1958, in which it poured all afternoon, a warm southern California day greeted both teams. Sunshine, nearly 80 degrees and haze hung overhead as 102,063

ABOVE: Ohio State quarterback Rex Kern confers with head coach Woody Hayes during the 1969 Rose Bowl. (Ohio State University Photo Archive)

fans packed the stadium while millions more watched on television.

The game typified the Buckeyes' surprising season. Following a scoreless first quarter, USC built a 10-0 lead in the second quarter thanks to a 21-yard field goal followed by an 80-yard touchdown run by Simpson.

Simpson's run could have destroyed a weaker team, but instead it galvanized the young Buckeyes. According to former quarterback Rex Kern: "Following O.J.'s run, I walked into the huddle and basically said, 'We've screwed around long enough…it's time for us to play.'"

Down 10-nothing, Ohio State fought back as Kern marched his team on a 13-play, 69-yard drive. Fullback Jim Otis and halfback Leo Hayden went over the tackles. Then Kern read a USC blitz by sending Hayden up the middle for 13. Ray Gillian grabbed a high pass for 18 more down to the three. Two plays later, Otis plunged in for the Buckeyes' first touchdown of the day. Jim Roman's extra point was good and OSU trailed, 10-7.

Late in the second quarter, Ohio State's defense held on a third and 13. USC then punted down to the Buckeyes' 40-yard line with a 1:04 left before the half. Ohio State drove 54 yards before stalling at USC's six-yard line. Roman booted a 26-yard field goal to tie the game at 10-10 with three seconds left in the half.

Halftime proved to be more interesting than the two great bands battling it out on the field. President-elect Richard Nixon watched the first half of the game with Ohio's governor, James Rhodes. He escorted Nixon to the center of the field to meet California governor Ronald Reagan, who then took Nixon and his party to watch the second half from the stands on the USC side of the field.

Ohio State's offensive unit opened the third quarter as it had ended the first half, by scoring. The Buckeyes used power football, running Otis and Hayden up the middle on USC's defense, putting together a 12-play drive that culminated in a 25-yard Roman field goal, giving OSU its first lead of the day, 13-10.

Ohio State's defense came out strong in the second half as well, frustrating O.J. Simpson by shutting down his running lanes while terrorizing quarterback Steve Sogge. The big break came in the fourth quarter when defensive tackle Bill Urbanik crushed Sogge, causing a fumble, which tackle Vic Stottlemeyer recovered at USC's 21. Then Kern, finding no open receivers, ran 17 yards down to the Trojans' four-yard line. Two plays later, Kern tossed a soft pass over the USC linebackers to a streaking Hayden for a score. Roman booted the extra point, and Ohio State now led, 20-10.

The young Buckeyes now had their swagger back, and the defense was starting to look like the team that shut down number one Purdue earlier in the season. Ohio State defensive back Mike Polaski recovered a Simpson fumble on USC's 16-yard line. On the very next play, Kern survived a Trojans blitz, hitting Gillian, who took it in for six more points before throwing the ball into the stands. Roman's extra point was good as Ohio State built an seemingly insurmountable 27-10 lead with 10:05 left to play.

Late in the game, USC scored a controversial touchdown that left Hayes howling mad. With 45 seconds remaining in the fourth quarter, Sogge tossed a high pass from OSU's 19-yard line into the end zone that Polaski apparently intercepted. But the officials ruled that Polaski, who had jumped to catch the pass, interfered with Trojan end Sam Dickerson, who had also jumped in an attempt to catch the ball.

Replays showed that both players grasped the ball together for an instant. Polaski then took full possession of the ball before coming down in the end zone for an apparent interception. The officials ruled that Dickerson had possession long enough, a millisecond, and ruled it a touchdown. When Hayes realized the officials had ruled that USC had scored a touchdown, he stormed the field, picking up a 15-yard penalty. USC's two-point conversion failed and the score stayed at 27-16, OSU.

The Trojans then tried an onside kick that was recovered by the Buckeyes. Two plays later, the clock ran out as Ohio State claimed its stake as the nation's top-ranked team by beating second-ranked USC, 27-16. The victory gave Ohio State a perfect 10-0 season, a national championship and its fourth undefeated-untied season in school history.

No one besides OSU linebacker Mark Stier will ever know the amount of pain that he played through that afternoon. Stier had suffered a separated shoulder in practice, two days prior to the Rose Bowl. With co-captain and linebacker Dirk Worden out with torn knee ligaments, Stier knew OSU couldn't afford to miss another leader on defense and conceded later: "It hurt quite a bit."

The Buckeyes' offense, which had started slowly, had 21 first downs compared to USC's 19. Ohio State ground out 260 yards to the Trojans' 177. Eighty of those yards came on a single Simpson touchdown run in the second quarter. The big difference was turnovers. The Buckeyes didn't commit a single turnover on the afternoon, while USC gave the ball away five times with three fumbles and two interceptions.

Otis had been the workhorse in the victory for the Buckeyes. The junior fullback carried the ball 30 times for 101 yards and a touchdown. Hayden carried the ball a surprising 15 times for 90 yards and a touchdown. Ray Gillian gained 14 yards on six carries while catching four passes for 69 yards, including one for a score.

The writers voted Kern as the game's Most Valuable Player after he completed nine of 15 passes for 101 yards and two touchdowns. He also carried the ball 12 times for 35 yards in the win.

According to former OSU middle guard Jim Stillwagon: "After we got back into the locker room, we all crowded around Coach Hayes and began the chanting 'One, One, One,' while holding up our first fingers. Then Simpson walked in and everyone got quiet. He was standing there all sweaty, in his red and gold uniform, and told us, 'You're the best team in the country, and don't let anybody tell you you aren't.' Then he raised two fingers over his head, showing us that the Trojans were number two, and walked out. It was great."

After Simpson left the locker room, Hayes announced that Kern had been named MVP. Paul Hornung of the *Columbus Dispatch* wrote: "Cheers bounced around the locker room again and teammates pummeled Rex. 'Don't hit him on this shoulder,' Woody pleaded, protecting Kern's left. 'It went out again today.'" Coach Hayes then said, "Every part of this belongs to you guys," waving the trophy around the room, "the greatest team in the nation."

Kern wasn't the only one hurting. Hayes then gave the game ball to center John Muhlbach, saying: "The little guy probably had his ankle fractured today." A groan went

"Every part of this [Rose Bowl trophy] belongs to you guys, the greatest team in the nation."

—Coach Woody Hayes

up from John's teammates. "Doggone it, he deserves it anyway." Zelina was also injured; he sat out the final three quarters with three cracked ribs, suffered early in the first quarter. Hayden, who pulled a leg muscle earlier in the week, gutted it out, rushing 15 times for 90 yards.

Like a swarm of locusts, the reporters descended around Coach Hayes, and he was asked what the single biggest play of the game was. Before he could respond, someone suggested Sogge's fumble in the second half. The *Columbus Dispatch* reported Hayes answered by saying: "I hate to put the rap on the kid, but I guess you could say that was a big play."

Hayes was also asked if this was his best team. He responded with, "It won its ninth game more decisively, but that '54 team was a fabulous team. We had some great runners on that team too, maybe not as many as we do now and not as much speed on the line. Our '61 team was awfully good too."

Later, after the other reporters had left, Hornung asked Hayes: "Was this your biggest victory?" Hayes answered: "I suppose it was. Pretty convincing, wasn't it? I was a little worried. We weren't sharp and we had Steir hurt and Rex's shoulder. But Mark played the whole game and Rex's should went out again, but he said it went right back in after he went

all the way." Two days later, Hayes became an unofficial U.S. envoy to servicemen in Vietnam and adjacent military installations, showing color movies of the 1969 Rose Bowl to anybody who was able to watch them as he described the action.

The 1969 Rose Bowl victory over USC capped a remarkable season that saw the young Buckeyes go 10-0, with wins over top-ranked Purdue, fourth-ranked Michigan, and with number two USC in giving OSU its first national title since the 1957 season. It would also be its last until the Buckeyes' magical run in 2002. The victory over USC re-established Ohio State as a force to be reckoned with for years to come.

SCORES BY QUARTER	1ST	2ND	3RD	4TH	TOTAL
Ohio State	0	10	3	14	27
USC	10	0	0	6	16

1st Q-(USC) Ayale 28-yd FG (3-0 USC)
1st Q-(USC) Simpson 80-yd TD (10-0 USC)
2nd Q-(OSU) Otis 1-yd TD (10-7 USC)
2nd Q-(OSU) Roman 26-yd FG (10-10)
3rd Q-(OSU) Roman 25-yd FG (13-10 OSU)
4th Q-(OSU) Kern to Hayden 4-yd TD pass (20-10 OSU)
4th Q-(OSU) Kern to Gillian 16-yd TD pass (27-10 OSU)
4th Q-(OSU) Sogge to Dickerson 19-yd TD pass (Ex. Point failed 27-16 OSU)

2003 FIESTA BOWL

OHIO STATE 31, MIAMI 24 (2OT)

Championships on any level are not given to teams because they've had great seasons. Teams earn their championships. Many outstanding seasons have been tossed by the wayside following a loss in a championship format. *College Football News* called the 2003 Fiesta Bowl matchup between number one Miami and second-ranked Ohio State the second greatest game in college football history, behind only the 1984 Orange Bowl game in which Miami beat Nebraska 31-28. For Buckeye fans, it will go down as the greatest game in Ohio State football history.

Ohio State entered the contest as 11 1/2-point underdogs to the reigning national champions, who had won 34 consecutive games. Most national experts and fans didn't give the Buckeyes a chance of defeating Miami, led by Heisman Trophy finalists quarterback Ken Dorsey and running back Willis McGahee.

The announced crowd of 77,502 attending the Fiesta Bowl in Tempe, Arizona, was treated to absolutely ideal weather conditions. Clear skies and 70 degrees with a slight wind out of the west greeted the players when kickoff occurred at 6:21 p.m. Mountain Time. With Hall of Fame baseball player Cal Ripken Junior helping out, Miami won the coin toss, but deferred and decided to kick off to Ohio State while defending the North goal.

Call it nerves, a good Hurricanes defense or a combination of the two, the Buckeyes'

offense went three and out in its first two series of the contest. Meanwhile, Miami had limited success offensively in its first series against the OSU defense before punting the ball back to the Buckeyes following nine plays.

With just over six minutes to go in the first quarter, the Hurricanes received the ball back from Ohio State following its second straight three and out series. Starting from its own 48-yard line, Miami marched 52 yards in five plays, scoring the first points of the game on a 25-yard touchdown pass from Ken Dorsey to Roscoe Parrish. The touchdown came on an OSU blitz, leaving three-time All-America safety Michael Doss in single coverage, Doss's Achilles' heel. The extra point was good for a seven-nothing Hurricanes lead.

Midway through the second quarter with Miami still leading 7-0 and Ohio State facing a fourth and one at Miami's 17-yard line, kicker Mike Nugent was sent in for a 34-yard chip-shot field goal attempt. Instead, the Buckeyes ran a fake, which was quickly snuffed out by the Hurricanes' special teams.

On the previous Miami drive, Ohio State had failed to capitalize on cornerback Dustin Fox's interception of Ken Dorsey. With Miami driving, Dorsey tossed his second interception of the contest. It went straight into the arms of safety Michael Doss, whom Dorsey had victimized earlier for the 'Canes first score of the night. Doss redeemed himself by returning the

(Jeff Brehm)

pick 35 yards down to the Miami 17-yard line. Seven plays later, Ohio State quarterback Craig Krenzel took the ball in from one yard out to give the Buckeyes their first points of the night. Mike Nugent booted the extra point to tie the score at 7-7 with 3:08 to play in the first half.

Following a touchback on the ensuing kickoff, Ohio State's defense made another statement to the powerful Hurricanes offense. On first and 10 from their own 20-yard line, quarterback Ken Dorsey fumbled the ball following a vicious sack by OSU defensive tackle Kenny Peterson. Teammate Darrion Scott recovered the fumble at Miami's 15-yard line. Two plays later, freshman running back Maurice Clarett took the ball in from seven yards out as the Buckeyes grabbed a 13-7 lead. Mike Nugent's second extra point try of the night was good for a 14-7 lead with 1:05 left before halftime.

By the time the first half ended, Ohio State's stalwart defense had picked off two of Ken Dorsey's passes and recovered one fumble while sacking him three times. The naysayers who had predicted a blowout before the game were quickly realizing Ohio State might have what it would take to knock off the defending national champions.

On the opening drive of the third quarter, Ohio State's defense picked up where it had left off, stopping Miami on a third and three at its own 27-yard line. Following a 43-yard punt by the Hurricanes, Ohio State began one of its biggest series of the season. Following two Maurice Clarett runs, a false-start penalty, another Clarett run and a pass to Clarett, quarterback Craig Krenzel unleashed his longest pass of the season. It was a 57-yard strike to receiver Chris Gamble, who was taken down at Miami's six-yard line.

With the Buckeyes on the verge of making this a 21-7 contest early in the third quarter, one of the biggest plays of the season was about to take place. On the very next play, Krenzel's first-down pass to tight end Ben Hartsock was intercepted in the end zone by safety Sean Taylor, who headed down the left sideline. With OSU running back Maurice Clarett in high-speed pursuit, Clarett stole the ball back for the Buckeyes at the Miami 28. Four plays later, Ohio State settled for a Mike Nugent 44-yard field goal to give the Buckeyes a 17-7 lead.

Late in the third quarter Miami bounced back with a seven-play 55-yard scoring drive culminating in a touchdown run from nine yards out by running back Willis McGahee. This cut the Ohio State lead down to 17-14. On the play, McGahee showed why he was a finalist for the 2002 Heisman Trophy Award. After taking the handoff from quarterback Ken Dorsey, he cut around his right end and scored a spectacular touchdown by crossing the goal line just inside of the sideline.

With the tension beginning to mount, both teams missed field goals to start the fourth quarter. Just when it seemed that Miami's ground attack had began to power-up, McGahee left the game after suffering a severe knee injury. Midway through the fourth quarter with the 'Canes moving the ball downfield, Dorsey found flanker Roscoe Parrish for 26 yards to the OSU 21, but cornerback Dustin Fox, who had earlier intercepted Dorsey, forced Parrish to fumble on a wicked tackle. Safety Will Allen recovered for the Buckeyes at their own 18-yard line. The clock now read 5:08 to play in the fourth quarter.

Trying to chew up the clock and keep possession of the ball, Ohio State fired off five

consecutive running plays, consuming nearly three minutes. On third and six at his own 32, Krenzel's attempted pass to receiver Chris Gamble fell incomplete. Roscoe Parrish then fielded Andy Groom's punt at his own 24-yard line. Parrish then ran the ball back 50 yards before being tackled by Groom and Doss at the OSU 26.

With only 2:02 showing on the clock, Ohio State's defense was called upon again to make a critical stop. Tailback Jarrett Payton, now playing for the injured Willis McGahee, gained one yard on first down. On second down, Simon Frazer sacked Dorsey for a five-yard loss. Dorsey's pass on third down to Payton gained seven yards, making it fourth and seven from Ohio State's 23. Following a Miami timeout with three seconds to play, the Hurricanes brought out kicker Todd Sievers to try to send the game into overtime. In an attempt to "ice" the kicker, OSU called two consecutive timeouts. Sievers, who had missed his last three attempts, including one earlier in the fourth quarter, booted the ball just inside the right upright as time expired, tying the contest at 17 and sending the game into the first overtime in Bowl Championship Series history.

If you suffered from a weak heart or lack of fortitude, the drama of the next several minutes was not for you. However, if you enjoy skydiving, racing a car around a track at 200 mph or entering a haunted house at Halloween, the overtime was right up your alley.

Ohio State won the toss and elected to start on defense in the overtime. With the ball placed at the stadium's south end at the 25-yard line, the Hurricanes needed just five plays to take the lead at 24-17. Dorsey's pass over the middle to tight end Kellan Winslow Jr. was spectacular as Winslow caught the ball while jumping and reaching over defender Will Allen.

With college football fans across the country glued to the edge of their seats, Ohio State had to answer with its own touchdown and extra point or the game would be over. A penalty and a sack put OSU in a do-or-die situation. Faced with a fourth and 14 from the 29, Krenzel completed a 17-yard pass to Michael Jenkins for a first down. Krenzel then ran it to the five-yard line, but OSU was again faced with a fourth down. On fourth and three at the Miami five-yard line, Krenzel's pass to Chris Gamble fell incomplete to the ground in the corner of the end zone.

The game was over. Fireworks exploded overhead while Miami's fans raced onto the field to celebrate with their team. But there was a flag on the field! Field judge Terry Porter had thrown his flag late and signaled pass interference on Miami's Glenn Sharp. "I replayed it in my mind," Porter said. "I wanted to make sure that it was the right call."

After security officials had cleared the field, Clarett proceeded to gain just one yard on two carries. Krenzel then followed his right guard into the end zone for six points. Following a false start penalty, which set the Buckeyes back five yards, Mike Nugent kicked the all-important extra point to tie the score at 24-24.

Ohio State started on offense after switching to the north end of the stadium. Five plays later Maurice Clarett scored his second touchdown of the night from five yards out to give OSU a 31-24 lead following Nugent's extra point.

Miami was now faced with something foreign. Instead of being the hunter, they had become the hunted. The pressure of a 34-game winning streak, 24-0 under head coach Larry Coker, trying to win a second consecutive national championship and facing one of the most dominant defenses in the country finally caught up to the Hurricanes.

Although Krenzel and Gamble were OSU's MVPs in 2002, middle linebacker Matt Wilhelm was selected as the Big Ten Conference's Most Valuable Player. According to Wilhelm, "Big-time players step up in big-time games," said former OSU linebacker Chris Spielman. "Matt knew what was on the line. Heck, the whole Ohio State defense knew." With Miami now forced to score a touchdown to send the game into a third overtime, Wilhelm and company stepped up to the challenge.

Wilhelm stopped Miami's Jarrett Payton on first down for a one-yard loss. Then Dorsey's throw to Kellen Winslow fell incomplete. In the process, Dorsey was shaken up following a tenacious rush that resembled a pack of dogs at a meat market and had to leave the field. Backup Derrick Crudup came in and completed an eight-yard pass on a third-and-11. Dorsey then returned and hit Winslow for seven yards on fourth down. That, coupled with a facemask penalty, gave Miami a first and goal from Ohio State's six-yard line. The Buckeyes were flagged on a second consecutive play for pass interference on an incomplete pass to Andre Johnson. The Hurricanes were now first and goal at the Buckeyes' two-yard line.

Payton gained a yard on first down, and Dorsey's pass to Winslow fell incomplete on second down. Matt Wilhelm met fullback Quadtrine Hill at the goal line on third down, setting up another do-or-die situation. It all came down to one play. For Miami, a chance to stay alive and force a third overtime. For Ohio State, a chance to win its first national championship since 1968. On fourth and goal at the OSU one, Dorsey dropped straight back to pass, but was pressured by an unblocked Cie Grant from the right side. Before Dorsey hit the ground he threw a desperation pass that fell incomplete, setting off the second celebration of the night, but the only one that counted as Ohio State held on to defeat Miami 31-24 in double overtime.

During a wild on-field celebration, Fiesta Bowl officials awarded Ohio State the 2003 Bowl Championship Series National Championship Trophy, OSU's first national championship since winning the 1969 Rose Bowl. For second-year head coach Jim Tressel, it was a season like no other.

"They're an incredible bunch of kids. They just kept playing. It's fourth down and they're making a play. You just can't say enough about the 13 seniors, a bunch of great coaches, other young kids willing to take the leadership of those two groups, can't say enough."

Ohio State junior quarterback Craig Krenzel was asked afterwards about the controversial fourth-down flag. Kreznel's response in the postgame press conference carried live on 1460, WBNS-AM, Columbus, Ohio: "After I threw that, I got hit. As I was getting hit and the ball was in the air, I saw a lot of contact going on in the corner, but after that I was laying on the ground. The ball fell incomplete and their team rushed the field and I just kind of sat there. It was just a feeling of dejection thinking that the game was over and knowing how hard we played, how much effort we put in and thinking that we weren't victorious. Yeah, I thought there was contact, but I didn't see the flag until after I got up. I think it was the right call, and fortunately, we capitalized on it."

For former Ohio State quarterback Rex Kern, who was part of the Buckeyes' last national championship some 34 years earlier, the victory over Miami put to bed a lot of personal demons: "This past season has put those two [1969 loss to Michigan, 1971 Rose Bowl loss to Stanford] losses on the back shelf, seeing our Buckeyes win the national championship this year. It's allowed me as an individual, I think for the first time in my life, to real-ly enjoy the magnitude of what the '68 season was to us as players. I mean it's incredible. That's probably been suppressed for 34 years because we're sophomores, we've got winter workouts, we've got spring ball and we've got our junior and senior years coming up. As a sophomore, playing the game at that time, winning the national championship, I don't ever think that I really experienced the emotions that go with winning the national championship."

While there have been big wins throughout the history of OSU football, none of the previous victories had as much pressure, scrutiny or as many people watching as the 2003 matchup with the Hurricanes.

I asked my radio partner Chris Spielman what he would have said in a pregame speech to the Buckeyes? Spielman's response: "Just win. There's your speech. Now go out and do it."

That says it all for Ohio State football fans: just win.

SCORES BY QUARTERS	1ST	2ND	3RD	4TH	OT	(2 OT)	TOTAL
Ohio State	0	14	3	0	7	7	31
Miami	7	0	7	3	7	0	24

1st Q-(Miami) Dorsey to Roscoe 25-yd TD (7-0 Miami)
2nd Q-(OSU) Krenzel 1-yd TD (7-7)
2nd Q-(OSU) Clarett 7-yd TD (14-7 OSU)
3rd Q-(OSU) Nugent 44-yd FG (17-7 OSU)
3rd Q-(Miami) McGahee 9-yd TD (17-14 OSU)
4th Q-(Miami) Sievers 40-yd FG (17-17)
1st OT-(Miami) Dorsey to Winslow 7-yd TD (24-17 Miami)
1st OT-(OSU) Krenzel 1-yd TD (24-24)
2nd OT-(OSU) Clarett 5-yd TD (31-24 OSU)

(Jeff Brehm)

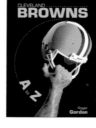

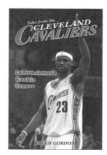